MAXWELL
PLAYS ONE

Glyn Maxwell

PLAYS ONE

THE LIFEBLOOD
WOLFPIT
THE ONLY GIRL IN THE WORLD

OBERON BOOKS
LONDON

First published in 2005 by Oberon Books Ltd
521 Caledonian Road, London N7 9RH
Tel: 020 7607 3637 / Fax: 020 7607 3629
e-mail: oberonbooks@btconnect.com
www.oberonbooks.com

A catalogue record for this book is available from the British Library.

ISBN: 1 84002 590 5

Cover design: Andrzej Klimowski

Printed and bound in Great Britain by Antony Rowe Ltd., Chippenham, Wilts

for James and Felicity Wren

And with special thanks to Greg Doran, Paul Garrington,
Bob Horwell, Guy Retallack, Sue Scott Davison,
Micheline Steinberg, Anthony Sycamore and Lloyd Trott.

Contents

Author's Note

- These plays are written in blank verse, so most of the lines are five-beat lines (or pentameters). Sometimes four-beat, three-beat or six-beat lines are used for various effects.

- Stage directions are kept to a minimum, and never is any indication given as to how a line should be said, but experience has taught one principle that should be insisted upon: any single line that is shared among two or more characters is still a single line. If spaces are allowed to intervene between the words of separate characters within a line the momentum is fatally harmed. These plays are composed of lines – not sentences or thoughts – and the lines should be kept intact.

- The indications as to ages or genders are guidelines based upon previous stagings; they are not strict instructions.

- All matters of design and costume are entirely in the hands of the producing company. Restricting a play to the historical period that merely forms its background can sometimes coat it with dust.

- Words and lines and spaces come where they come for a reason, as in a musical score. There is nothing poetic about these plays aside from that one principle of their construction. They are written in verse not for reasons of aesthetics or culture or nostalgia, but because poets write in verse and a poet wrote these.

THE LIFEBLOOD

'And because I dread the tyranny of those to whose power you have abandoned me, I entreat you not to permit that execution be done on me without your own knowledge…'

Letter of Mary to Elizabeth.

'God preserve me from making such a pitiable shipwreck of my conscience, or leaving so foul a stain on my posterity, as to shed blood without the authority of the law, and without a public act…'

Sir Amyas Paulet's response to Sir Francis Walsingham's suggestion, made on behalf of Queen Elizabeth, that he 'find some way of putting [Mary] to death'.

'Madame, the Queen my mistress, finds it very strange that you, contrary to the pact and engagement made between you, should have conspired against her and her State… And as you know that some of your servants are guilty, you will not take it ill that they are separated from you.'

Sir Thomas Gorges, at the arrest of Mary 'under colour of hunting'.

'I fear greatly that Nau [Arno] has hastened my death, having kept some papers, and [he is a man] who will turn on any side for [his] own advantage… I think they are making a scaffold to make me play the last scene of the Tragedy…'

Mary's letter to the Spanish Ambassador, after her arrest.

'Not one of them was favourable to your cause. And everyone else is astonished to see you so calm under the circumstances in which you find yourself. No living person has ever been accused of crimes so frightful and odious as yours.'

Paulet's response to Mary's contention that some of the men who tried her were sympathetic to her. Of the fifty judges, one alone declared himself 'not entirely satisfied' she was guilty.

'It is impossible to read without admiration, in the minute records of the trial, the self-possessed, prompt, clear, and sagacious replies and remarks, by which this forlorn woman defended herself against the most expert lawyers and politicians of the age; who, instead of examining her as judges, pressed her with the unscrupulous ingenuity of enemies.'

Sir James Mackintosh, 1905.

'I did not expect such a happy end. You do me honour in considering me a necessary instrument for the re-establishing of religion in this island.'

Mary's response to the reading of the warrant for her execution.

Characters

MARY STUART
formerly Queen of Scotland

CLAUDE ARNO
her secretary

SIR THOMAS GORGE
a government agent

SIR AMYAS PAULET
a Puritan gentleman

SIR FRANCIS WALSINGHAM
a Minister of the Crown

SIR WILLIAM CECIL

SIR THOMAS BROMLEY

SIR CHRISTOPHER HATTON
Commissioners trying the Queen

The action takes place in 1587–88.

Note: the rôles may be conveniently doubled thus:

ARNO / BROMLEY
GORGE / HATTON
PAULET / CECIL

This play was first performed in August 2001 at the Hen and Chickens Theatre Bar, London with the following cast:

MARY, Felicity Wren
ARNO, Andrew Wale
PAULET, Gerard McDermott
GORGE, Alun Maxwell
WALSINGHAM, Chris Gilling

Director, Paul Garrington
Designer, Nicky Shaw
Produced by James Wren for Unrestricted View
in association with Toye.

This revised version of the play was first performed at The Caves, at Edinburgh Festival 2004 and at Wiltons Music Hall, London with the following cast:

MARY, Sue Scott Davison
ARNO, Peter Hamilton Dyer
PAULET, Paul Goodwin
GORGE, Henry Luxemburg
WALSINGHAM, Chris Gilling

Director, Guy Retallack
Designer, Dora Schweitzer
Produced by Sue Scott Davison for Lifeblood Theatre Co.
in association with Gilded Balloon.

Act One

(*Dawn. Rain. MARY writing. ARNO comes.*)

MARY: 'Two miserable small rooms, which had I not
    entrenched about with tapestries of mine,
    I scarce could stay in for the damp and cold
    I daily breathe.' Daily I breathe?

ARNO: My lady,
    we have to speak.

MARY: Daily I breathe is right,
    yes? or as it is: I daily breathe?

ARNO: I daily breathe, *c'est ca.*

MARY: My daily breath,
    that's it, give us this day our daily breath!
    I have it, Claude. 'Two miserable small rooms...'

ARNO: My lady, if I may...

MARY: They *are* miserable,
    they *are* small, aren't they? When I was a child
    no room was ever small. I ought to write that.
    If she, for a moment only, my dear sister,
    could see this foul allotment
    she'd burn for shame.

ARNO: *Bien sur, bien sur.* My lady,
    I do have news to tell you.

MARY: Claude has news,
    news of the rain quickening, news of owls,
    news of the English language turning round
    its back to me, no doubt, for all the good
    these letters do.

ARNO: It is about the letters.

MARY: I have it, I have solved it. I have written
    all these years in hieroglyphs. I write
    to my dear sister I am in despair,
    then all her ministers translate it thus:
    'Heigh-ho, another dawn, another day!
    Life is sweet between my icy pillow
    and the sewage in the yard, only this morning

Claude trod in it and splashed me, how we chuckled!'
I don't want any news.
ARNO: You want this news.
MARY: I don't believe in news. I have become
a pagan to the news. But my kneebones ache,
I must have knelt to something. In my sleep
I knelt and knew the gift of rheumatism.
You know why else I'm aching? Guess, Claude.
ARNO: I can't –
MARY: Guess, *devinez*.
ARNO: You haven't slept.
MARY: I never sleep, no prizes.
I ache because I'm growing. Have you thought
our rooms get smaller? So it looked to you,
but it's us, Claude, we're growing. When I leave,
I'll burst the walls and pick the Queen of England
gently from the flowerbed of London,
I'll pocket her and pat her for forgiveness.
I don't want any news. I want instead…
that you assist me where it matters, Claude.
I've this about Sir Amyas: 'Our host',
shall I say, 'generous host'?
ARNO: But it isn't true.
MARY: She may laugh, though, I think she'll laugh.
ARNO: *Peut-etre.*
MARY: *Peut-etre.* Well… 'My host has from the first
with harshness and indignity beset me…'
That's fair, no? 'Harshness and indignity.'
I think Sir Amyas would be quite delighted
at 'harshness and indignity'.
ARNO: My news
concerns Sir Amyas.
MARY: Listen. It gets better.
'Indeed he is more suited for a jailer
of thieves or murderers. And I believe
my life is not secure in this man's care.'
ARNO: You've written that? We have assurances.
MARY: You hear the birds? They differ in opinion.
I haven't slept. Where's Jane?

ARNO: My lady,
   there is a man…

MARY: They hold it back, the sparrows,
   they know what daybreak means to me,
   they're sorry when they start.

ARNO: There is a man
   who's come from Paris, from Morgan...

MARY: Morgan… In France…

ARNO: Stopped by me in the yard,
   this man, he used the cipher. He's here.

MARY: One of our people, Claude?

ARNO: One of your people.

MARY: One of my people. Out there, in the yard?
   On earth?

ARNO: When Sir Amyas comes to us this morning,
   take your walk alone.

MARY: There's no alone.
   Sir Amyas drifts behind me like a shadow.
   I'd have to leave the earth to shake him off.

ARNO: You walk alone, Sir Amyas has to walk,
   allowing me a moment with this stranger.
   So I converse with him. So I can test him
   with the old cipher. Do you understand this?

MARY: The old cipher… Yes – why, yes, you do that.
   You have to forgive me, Claude, it's been so long
   since anything went better than the day
   before it, now I'm dizzy. Do you think
   I reached a place so dark that only light
   can follow now?

ARNO: I'll meet him.
   I'll test him. But I think he's – of our mind.

MARY: To be of our mind, Claude, requires you live
   eighteen years under a slanting ceiling.
   And it requires a blink to cross a room,
   and it requires the window that you gaze through
   is smaller when you reach it than it was
   when you intended to. I'm going to bed,
   if no one's confiscated it. Where's Jane?

ARNO: I haven't heard her. The house is very quiet.

MARY: Quiet as things so small they have lost voices.
All the lights are out. Nobody's coming.
(*MARY goes. ARNO looks out for the 'stranger'. PAULET comes.*)

PAULET: Where is your mistress? Are there letters for me?

ARNO: There are never letters for you. There are letters
my mistress writes in private, which you read.

PAULET: I read them on the orders of my mistress.

ARNO: They're chiefly *to* your mistress. When she eats
I'm sure you tell her when it's time to taste.

PAULET: Where is she now?

ARNO: The Queen is gone to bed.
You frown. Is sleep allowed? Are dreams allowed?
Do you require reports of dreams?

PAULET: This lady
is not a queen. You know that, but deny it
like a man condemned.

ARNO: And would do if I were one.
Her dream, I can report,
is of a bluebell meadow, which in time
a man in a hat sets fire to. And are yours
of a wild blaze and a poor lady running?

PAULET: My dreams are of the Lord.

ARNO: So are my dreams.
He often mentions you. Yes, that's exactly
the kind of face He pulls.

PAULET: You are a fool.

ARNO: Not in the dream. I'm valued in the dream.
Why is the house so quiet?

PAULET: The house is quiet
because it was too loud and for too long.
The servants are dismissed.

ARNO: That's ludicrous.
She needs a household.

PAULET: This house has a household.
Her people are uncalled-for. They're not servants,
they are associates, familiars.

They spoke in riddles and they are dismissed.
They left for Scotland in the night, escorted.

ARNO: A simple English cruelty.

PAULET: An act
commanded, Monsieur Arno, not an impulse.

ARNO: She begs in English and the English Crown
takes all she has.

PAULET: I am no politician,
monsieur, I am a gentleman required
to guard this person –
(*MARY comes.*)

MARY: That's a voice that daily
pesters me in sleep.

ARNO: It's not good news.

MARY: Good news, I'm sure it isn't, for I would not
recognise good news if it approached me.
I'd think it had got lost, and would direct it
elsewhere with a smile.

ARNO: This Christian
has sent your staff away.

PAULET: I have obeyed
a royal command.

MARY: My staff?
You sent them where?

ARNO: To Scotland,
they left last night.

MARY: My staff?
Who's left?

PAULET: This man remains,
as does your doctor.

MARY: One man to revive me,
one to write: 'The lady / is revived.'

PAULET: / Madam Stuart,
is the command unclear?

MARY: It's very clear.
I see clear through it like I see clear through
your meanest word. You sent my dears away
without goodbye. Of what are you composed?
Send back for them.

PAULET: Impossible.
MARY: Of course,
   impossible if where I have a heart
   you have a rail. You relish my discomfort.
PAULET: That's nonsense. I am bearing out a duty,
   Madam Stuart.
MARY: This isn't from my sister.
PAULET: You have no sister.
MARY: From my sister queen.
PAULET: You are no queen.
MARY: I was anointed one,
   you spineless little sentry.
PAULET: I may indeed –
MARY: You may indeed do nothing.
   I am an anointed queen. The King of France
   I married and I reigned a queen in Scotland.
   Whatever state the ministers of London
   reduce me to, or set you like a dog
   to bark at, don't you dare forget these eyes
   stare through you with the eyes of generations.
PAULET: And you would be as well –
MARY: Can you not see me?
   Did I indicate you had a cue to speak?
   Your sovereign's blood is mine. Your queen and I
   originate as sisters in King Henry.
   Do Puritans read history? I doubt it.
   They'd hear too many songs the world's still singing.
PAULET: Madam –
MARY: I shall write further to my sister.
   I shall exempt her, as I know that man,
   that Walsingham's to blame, him I was warned of.
PAULET: Write what you will to whom you will. All letters
   pass before my eyes.
MARY: The ink is acid,
   so read them closely, do. Now, go away.
PAULET: I'll leave you to your history-making then.
   – And a spineless man would never have been shouldered
   with such a burden as your *entourage*.

(*PAULET goes. MARY takes out her letter.*)

MARY: Look. And I spent the night in telling her
    how dreadfully I'm treated. Now it seems
    I'm to be made nostalgic for the life
    I raged about three hours ago. My friends!

ARNO: They don't believe in friends.

MARY: They took the coachmen.

ARNO: Or in seeing the world.

MARY: We're going nowhere.
    Unless they find a smaller house, perhaps
    one bed, Claude, between us, or a barn.
    And no more journeys. All the things I love,
    uprooted from the ground. So I'll grow more.
    Roses I'll grow.

ARNO: In the meantime,
    my lady, take your walk.

MARY: So take my arm.

ARNO: I wish to, I would always wish to do so,
    my lady, but remember, he must watch you,
    Sir Amyas, he can't let you walk unwatched,
    and I may therefore –

MARY: Oh, I see, your man,
    your stranger, Claude. I thought you'd found yourself
    a better walking partner. I was jealous,
    wasn't I? I thought I'd lost you too!

ARNO: You never shall.

MARY: I thought they'd plucked you too,
    just think, my loyal Claude!

ARNO: They never shall.

MARY: No, I can see that, here. So. Now I'll walk,
    my secretary a light at the high window,
    my Puritan a puddle to avoid.
    Sun and rain, life shrinking to the weather.
    Where are we?

ARNO: Where *are* we?

MARY: You said it.

ARNO: Stafford.

MARY: Stafford. Stafford shire. Make a fair copy,   (*Letter.*)
 there's more to come, as always. Stafford shire.
 Even the names are forms of punishment.
 (*MARY goes, leaving ARNO with her letter. He reads it.*
 GORGE is there.)

GORGE: Staffordshire. Fair point.

ARNO: I didn't see you.

GORGE: I wasn't there. Keep her in your eyeline.
 I've got the Puritan.

ARNO: He has his servants.

GORGE: I have them too. They are unloading kegs.
 One of them's giving orders. In my eye
 he stands an inch but he's the man in charge.
 They are all accounted for.

ARNO: The man you came from…

GORGE: I came from a woman, sir. Just now in fact.

ARNO: I mean, who sent you – does the man who sent you
 know the Psalms?

GORGE: He knows the fifth and seventh.

ARNO: Is that all?

GORGE: Yes.

ARNO: He has no preference?
 Then I don't know you.

GORGE: Claude, he likes the twelfth.
 Just testing.

ARNO: As was I.
 Your name?

GORGE: You must be joking.

ARNO: I was, of course.

GORGE: I laughed. Don't look at me.
 Look at the Queen.

ARNO: I've got her. Where's Paulet?

GORGE: I've got him, with arms folded. I can see
 the servants, and the beer. They're very jolly.
 I see the brewer himself. He works for me.
 Him it was who showed me that a beer-keg
 has a safe compartment. Can you see the Queen?

ARNO: She seemed to look up here, as if to find me.

GORGE: Then duck, we don't want that. Come where it's darker.
    Don't look at me. A dry compartment, Claude,
    in a beer-keg.
ARNO: Beer-keg?
GORGE: Are you a beer-man,
    monsieur? The yellow ciphers.
ARNO: The yellow ciphers, yes?
GORGE: Are they written down?
ARNO: They're in my head.
GORGE: Well, keep them there, or else
    they'll saw it off and have themselves a look.
    You see the Queen? Nod. Good. I see Paulet.
    Only his dog's in earshot, and his dog's
    a catholic of old. I work for Morgan.
    If there is anyone in Rome, or France,
    or Spain, with whom she might like to converse
    in privacy, write in the yellow ciphers,
    seal up the letter, find me.
    I stow them in the kegs and they go out.
    You following this, Claude? Don't look at me.
    What goes out can come in. This is the first.   (*A letter.*)
    True it smells of beer, but it's Staffordshire,
    everybody does.
ARNO: This is a letter
    Paulet hasn't seen?
GORGE: *I* haven't seen it,
    where is it? Gone! This is a private letter,
    remember, from the old world,
    from one fine London gentleman I know
    by reputation, to the Queen of Scotland.
    Your nose will be the first to burrow in it.
    Don't breathe too sharply, will you. Your next home
    could be a room you have to die to exit.
ARNO: Sir, we have these many years read letters
    from desperate men, from madmen. If my lady
    had given them encouragement in writing,
    no mercy could have saved her. We have never
    thought it wise to act –

GORGE: Time to start thinking.
     I live out there, I feel how the wind's blowing.
     We have to get her out of England, Claude.
     Elizabeth's soft heart,
     that's all that's keeping her in…in the pink.
     Read the letter.
ARNO: What? I've lost the Queen…
     (*GORGE has gone. ARNO reads the letter. WALSINGHAM
     appears, reading the same letter.*)
WALSING: 'Myself in person, with ten gentlemen,
     and a hundred others of our company,
     will undertake the glorious deliverance
     of your Royal Person from your enemies.
     And, as regards the question of removal
     of that usurper from your English throne,
     there are six gentlemen of quality,
     who, for the love they bear our Catholic cause,
     stand ready to accomplish the design…'

Act Two

MARY: It's you!

ARNO: It is, are you surprised, my lady?

MARY: I jumped, yes.

ARNO: Was I so unexpected?
   Is what you're writing secret from your servant?

MARY: Oh, not at all, I was so far away
   in writing it, the world seemed to be less,
   less to remember, less to touch – look, Claude,
   I'm signing it, I have a shadow-letter
   for your shadow-man to carry –

ARNO: Not my man,
   Morgan's man, but verified by me.

MARY: Verified, oh yes…you know, my answer
   wrote itself! It finished in my mind
   before my hand moved. Eighteen years I yearned
   for privacy. Now when I write words
   I show my heart, you see?

ARNO: I have been thinking,
   my lady, very hard about the letter,
   the letter from this –

MARY: Anthony.

ARNO: *Quand-même.*
   He hopes to serve you, and at least believes
   he has support both here –

MARY: He says he served me
   as a boy.

ARNO: He did, I know the name.

MARY: Anthony.

ARNO: *Quand-même.* In Shrewsbury's house.

MARY: I don't recall, unless he was that page
   who drank the dregs of wine I left, was that him?
   A loyal servant.

ARNO: If your memory serves you.
   He seems a daring gentleman –

MARY: If it takes
    a daring gentleman to win my freedom,
    a daring gentleman is what we're seeking.
    Is there wine anywhere?
ARNO: I'll fetch the wine.
    I'll be the daring secretary who does that.
MARY: And this came in a beer-box.
ARNO: A beer-keg.
MARY: A beer-keg, then hidden in the pocket
    of our shadow-friend, our mystery visitor!
    He must know Anthony! The brave are here
    in Staffordshire!
ARNO: Yes, hiding in beer-boxes.
MARY: It's beer-keg.
ARNO: Accept this sorry wineglass,
    nothing hidden.
MARY: Ha! But I'll still check!
    No messages for me! I've been forgotten!
ARNO: My lady, no. His – letter gives us heart,
    of course it does, it shows how you are loved,
    supported, prayed for, dreamed of, but –
MARY: But what?
ARNO: It's, don't you think, it's full of heat, it's more,
    more passionate than anything, it's more
    emotional –
MARY: Monsieur,
    heat is required here, passion's welcome,
    love is longed for!
ARNO: Love,
    my lady? He might be a man in love.
MARY: And a man in love might be a man I need.
    Is love a field in which you are well-versed?
    Is that what you've been studying by firelight?
    Did you qualify? Are you going to give me lessons?
    A gentleman in love may be a soldier,
    a warrior.
ARNO: Or he – may be a fool.
MARY: Or he may be a fool. Am I a fool?
    What did this fool do next?

ARNO: You're not a fool.
　　Consult the Ambassador, the Duke your uncle.
　　Now you can talk in secret, you can learn
　　the truth of what's out there. This daring soul,
　　this Anthony Babington, let's learn exactly
　　whom he knows –
MARY: You met the beer-keg man,
　　Claude, you told me I could write my heart out,
　　in secret, to this man, this gallant man
　　who knew me, who will risk his life, he wrote,
　　and I am writing back – now you are saying –
ARNO: Now I am saying 'wait', that's all I'm saying.
MARY: That's all you're saying, that's all you're always saying.
　　Well. I'm writing. Yes. Well, I shan't send it
　　if Claude is saying 'wait', that's not allowed,
　　I'll write it for, for – literature, *voilà,*
　　my contribution. Give it to some monks,
　　and they can illustrate it, in green ink.
ARNO: Keep it safe, my lady. We may need it,
　　they will not search you.
MARY: Will they not? How kind.
ARNO: All I say is wait until we know.
MARY: In the world of men I think that makes you wise,
　　and me a fool, and that's the world we're locked in.
　　Madame La Folie. This English wine
　　is frightful.
ARNO: Isn't it just?
　　This…Babington. This *design*
　　he speaks of is –
MARY: I know what the *design*
　　refers to, Claude.
ARNO: Assassination!
MARY: Young men
　　write what they have to write. If he will free me,
　　then I am free. What else he and his friends
　　design is their design, not my design.
ARNO: The men who need to do so will connect them.
MARY: This wine is truly English. I did think
　　one wasn't meant to notice poison.

ARNO: My lady,
    I drink before you drink.
MARY: Well then you'll die
    before me, I'll be lonely *and* thirsty.
    He drank the dregs I left, you know, I saw him,
    it's flooding back, he was a faithful boy.
    Well. He writes his letter, I write mine.
    Claude won't let it out into the world,
    so it can flutter here, like a love-token.
    Bon, I can hear my heart.
ARNO: That's gladdening.
MARY: I'll drink the dregs! There, now that's the daring
    of an old lady, Claude, that's what you've left me.
    What is desire in this world? Not a good thing.
    Look at this life that did what it desired.
    Better wait till doomsday with a glass
    of something that was sour till it was empty.
    Is that an English custom?
ARNO: My lady.
    My one desire is that what you desire,
    my lady, can be done – you know I am yours
    to the end of – to the end –
MARY: Well to the end
    of that sentence at least. That wise sentence.
    It's clouded over now. As a little girl
    I wished on one particular evening star.
    Well. Nothing ever comes of it but night time.
    There…not even dregs. Leave me, Claude.
    I have my letter. When I've written forty
    you can make a coat of them, a paper coat
    to sleep in while we're waiting.
    (*ARNO goes. WALSINGHAM and PAULET.*)
WALSING: She did what?
PAULET: Baptized a child, your grace.
    Last week, of a young woman in her household,
    a household much reduced upon your orders,
    and now –
WALSING: Reduced? How has it been reduced?
    It's been augmented, hasn't it, by the child?

30

PAULET: Both child and mother have departed.

WALSING: What,
   Staffordshire, or the earth?

PAULET: The house, your grace.
   Only two remain in her entourage.

WALSING: *Entourage.* Is that a word she taught you?

PAULET: I – no – why, no –

WALSING: It's just it's a French word.
   You might have learned it in your conversations.
   You have long conversations, so I've heard.
   Conversions?

PAULET: I try hard
   to shun these conversations, but the woman
   will persist in speaking, lecturing, I might say,
   as if I were a schoolboy.

WALSING: What did she call it?

PAULET: Pardon, your grace?

WALSING: What did she baptize it,
   Jean? Francois? Francoise? Was it *une fille*?

PAULET: I didn't ask.

WALSING: You didn't. Don't you care?
   Find out. It's good to know. Then for a moment
   you would have known a thing I don't know. Yes?
   That's power in this world, that's what it's made of.
   So they're allowed to do that in their faith.
   Without a priest?

PAULET: These acts are to my soul
   abominations, but they're of a piece
   with all her many wrongs. It is not allowed
   in England, nor permitted under God.

WALSING: Are there readers?

PAULET: Pardon?

WALSING: Readers.
   People who read. Do Puritans not read?
   What *do* you do? She used to smuggle priests in
   under pretext of reading.

PAULET: There are none.
   She has her secretary, and her doctor.

No visitor has access to her now.
She is restricted to the house and yard.
WALSING: Does she have books? You know, these things. Books.
PAULET: Too many books. She reads the chronicles
and draws from these fantastical conclusions
favouring her in all. I find her discourse
vexing and unwomanly.
WALSING: I hear
she cut you down to size.
PAULET: I beg your pardon?
WALSING: I said I hear she cut you down to size.
PAULET: I shall destroy her books.
WALSING: Do no such thing.
Leave the books alone. Leave her the books.
Keep her inside. If the sun does ever shine
make reasons why she can't go out. When it rains
then she can trudge her circles. Winter clothes.
Does she have winter clothes?
PAULET: I find her wardrobe
inappropriate and extravagant.
WALSING: Extravagant, or extravagant to you?
You mean she has two coats, don't you, two hats.
The symbols of her claims?
PAULET: Her 'Cloth of State'
still hangs above the bed.
WALSING: Well then remove it.
Her son. Does she ever mention him?
PAULET: Her son?
WALSING: Her son, the King of Scotland, Sir Amyas.
Women are mothers sometimes, it's been known
in worlds less puritan. He's signed a treaty.
This will upset her somewhat.
PAULET: She believes
he loves her still, regardless.
WALSING: Does she think that?
I love my mother, though. But then she's gone,
we both can be regardless. That's all.
PAULET: Begging you, your grace –
WALSING: She died at Easter.

PAULET: Pardon, your grace. The man I was informed
    would visit has, has visited. The hours
    he keeps are strange, his presence is unsettling.
    I do not think –
WALSING: You're not required to think.
    I said a man would visit. Let him visit.
    Stay in your place. Don't turn the page and look.
    You may not find your name. Do you understand?
    Are you not being remunerated?
PAULET: Richly,
    that is, proportionately, but it's not easy.
WALSING: The Queen is well aware of Sir Amyas Paulet.
PAULET: You – honour me.
WALSING: You honour her. In fact,
    I saw her just this morning, and she told me
    to let 'Sir Amyas' know that his good office
    is borne in mind. Her Majesty quite softly
    spoke of Sir Amyas.
PAULET: I am lost for words.
WALSING: Which is the way I like it. Go that way.
    (*Music. MARY writing. GORGE in shadow. He coughs.*)
MARY: You've caught another cold, Claude, or perhaps
    my poem is finished and you made the sound
    of English words affronted.
    (*Reads.*) 'Alas what am I? What use has my life?
    I am but a body whose heart's torn away,
    A vain shadow, an object of misery
    Who has nothing left but death-in-life.
    O my enemies, set your envy all aside;
    I've no more…' – is it good?
GORGE: It's very good so far.
    Is it going to be a sonnet?
MARY: When it ends
    it will be.
GORGE: I'll believe it when it ends then.
MARY: Claude, you've drunk some English beer. Who are you?
    (*GORGE steps into view.*)
GORGE: A sonnet lover. How many lines in sonnets?

MARY: Fourteen, of course. I don't think you're a poet.

GORGE: No, your royal highness, I count things.

MARY: You count things. You count me a royal highness?

GORGE: A glorious majesty. If the four walls
    weren't glued with eyes and ears of Puritans
    I'd kneel and say my name.

MARY: Well. They are, which spares your knees and throat.
    You are the stranger.

GORGE: So my mother said.

MARY: You are the beer-keg man. You are the man
    from Anthony. Monsieur –

GORGE: Monsieur is reading
    his own memoirs, which is his delight
    in the small hours.

MARY: Where's Sir Amyas Paulet?

GORGE: He is in London. I believe he sniffed
    a celebration somewhere in Smithfield
    and went to stamp it out.

MARY: Yes…that's Amyas,
    he dreamt of children dancing round a maypole,
    and it shocked him to the core.

GORGE: He heard a bird sing
    and rode to Parliament to get the law changed.

MARY: That's him, you know him well!

GORGE: Inseparable,
    we are, blood brothers. When he cracks a joke
    all England splits its side.

MARY: You're quite amusing,
    for a beer-keg man.

GORGE: Your majesty, you're cheerful
    for a captive audience.

MARY: I was born cheerful.
    I don't know why. It isn't even true.
    Why have you come to me? My Monsieur Arno
    does everything.

GORGE: He does? Does he write sonnets?

MARY: Yes. I write them and he writes them out.

GORGE: A secretary, then, not a sonneteer.

MARY: No, I'm the sonneteer. What's your business?
What's your name?

GORGE: My business is with you.
My name is with my mother, and my mother's
with the Lord. My lady, have you read
the letter –

MARY: Yes, from Anthony, you know
Anthony?

GORGE: I do, a noble soul.

MARY: Yes, is he?

GORGE: And a brave man, and a bold one.

MARY: I knew that from the letter.

GORGE: Was the letter
interesting to you?

MARY: I had replied
in a moment here, ten minutes here, and an hour...:
here.   (*Heart; head; letter.*)
(*ARNO comes.*)

ARNO: What are you doing?

GORGE: Sorry we woke you. Nothing to copy out yet.

MARY: Claude, your shadow's turned into a man.
He's come from Anthony.

ARNO: Do you have news?

GORGE: No.

ARNO: What do you have?

GORGE: About fourteen lines.

MARY: Your shadow heard my sonnet. He's my first
audience in England.

ARNO: Is he now.

GORGE: It's a fine poem, Claude. It has some rhymes,
some rhythms. Now be careful you don't spill them
in the copying out.

ARNO: My lady, her royal highness,
means to consult in general with those
most dear to her, prior to –

GORGE: When the hail
starts falling from the sky, do you consult
those most dear to you? Me, I just scarper.

ARNO: *C'est entre nous, n'est-ce pas, c'est un accord?*

MARY: Well. Claude advises me, and I,
　　I need him. He saves me from myself.

GORGE: My royal highness, it is not yourself
　　you need to be saved from.

ARNO: 　　　　　　　　　She will not reply
　　impulsively.

MARY: 　　　And you will not decree,
　　Claude, what I will do, impulsively
　　or otherwise.

ARNO: 　　　　*Pardonnez-moi.*

GORGE: 　　　　　　　　In English.

MARY: Is it your own opinion that this plan
　　of Babington's is, *qu'est-ce que c'est que ça,*
　　supported?

GORGE: 　　　It is massively supported.
　　No Catholic in England or in Europe
　　will stand by while you suffer here. The word
　　is everywhere. The fleets of France and Spain
　　are facing north.

MARY: 　　　　　My letter faces south, then.

ARNO: No!

MARY: 　　But I am steady,
　　I wait for the Ambassador's advice,
　　and that of the Duke my uncle.

GORGE: Right. And have they promised to inform you
　　when the lightning leaves the sky?

MARY: 　　　　　　　　　You shadow-man,
　　go back in shadow. If you wish to serve me,
　　serve me less of your English wit.

ARNO: 　　　　　　　　Indeed.
　　You shall receive our answer in good time.

GORGE: Time isn't good, *monsieur.* – I'm sorry. English.
　　I'm just a shadow, I can't help myself.
　　There's a light along the ridge. A single lantern
　　keeps the sky black. Puritan sunrise.
　　(*GORGE goes.*)

MARY: Well. I find your beer-keg man amusing.

ARNO: He has a certain, beer-keg manner. It seems
    he's licensed to be here and there and nowhere.

MARY: Everyone is but us. To meet that man
    is to have felt a breeze of to and fro.
    The freedom sickens me.

ARNO: It sickens me.

MARY: A secretary then. Not a sonneteer.

ARNO: *Pardonnez-moi?*

MARY: *En anglais.*
    Look, I place my heart back in its cage.   (*The letter.*)
    You hear it lock?

ARNO: It's Paulet at the gate.
    Returned from London.

MARY: Only when he heard
    my heart leap in the Midlands. London. *London.*
    Have you ever seen it?

ARNO: Yes. It isn't Paris.

MARY: Truly? I was hoping it was Paris.
    I'd see my dog, if it was long ago.
    I'd see my cousins in the early morning
    in a wood we had, we called the wood of shapes.
    But what there is is London.
    (*PAULET comes.*)

MARY: Good morning, Amyas. You forgot the sun.
    Did you leave it over the hill?

PAULET: I was in Westminster,
    on government state business.

MARY: Oh. Aren't I
    government state business?

PAULET: There is news.

MARY: You have a coat on, you're an angry man
    home from a journey: how could there not be news?

PAULET: Madam, none I know, who have observed you,
    can comprehend the levity with which
    you look upon the world.

MARY: And none I know
    would comprehend the gravity with which
    you scratch your elbow, Amyas. Well perhaps
    those we know lack skill in comprehension.

PAULET: A treaty has been signed. Do I smell beer?

MARY: Do you? I don't know. Have you been drinking?

PAULET: I do not drink, madame.

MARY: Of course you don't.
   For your faith is constructed out of feathers,
   and no one better laugh out loud.

ARNO: What treaty?

PAULET: A treaty has been signed.

ARNO: Yes. Concerning?

MARY: Don't spoil it, Claude, he wants it to take hours.

PAULET: Concerning England and concerning Scotland.

MARY: Concerning highland or concerning lowland,
   Amyas, be specific.

PAULET: King James,
   the King of Scotland, your son, Madam Stuart…

MARY: I don't know, have I met him? I don't think so.

PAULET: …has signed, to the great happiness of both
   these ancient realms, a Treaty of Alliance
   with our Royal Queen Elizabeth of England.

MARY: My sister-queen. Of course.
   Well. Of course, my son, and my dear sister,
   of course, in time, a treaty, it's no great
   news to us. Is it, Claude? No great
   surprise.

ARNO: I must confess –

MARY: We saw it coming.
   Two crowns, two ancient realms. You woke us up
   with this, Sir Amyas? You could still be sleeping.

PAULET: I thought you'd want to know.

MARY: You could be sleeping,
   still, tucked up, or dancing round, in Smithfield,
   dancing round the maypole.

PAULET: There will be
   between these realms renewed cooperation,
   two crowns will act as if a single mind.
   It is a glorious outcome. Good morning.
   (*PAULET goes. MARY is in shock.*)

ARNO: I didn't see that coming.

MARY: Say you did.
    Pretend you did. I'm pretending that I did.
    Then I can breathe.
ARNO: In retrospect, of course,
    it makes a certain kind of... The sun's rising.
MARY: The sun's rising. Well. Did you see that coming?
    I didn't. Well. Sweet Jesus, you keep watch,
    Claude, in *retrospect.* The sun's rising.
    Let me know its movements. Have it tailed.
    Where's my beer-keg man?
ARNO: It's an alliance
    of convenience.
MARY: Is that right, monsieur?
    That's interesting. Sun still rising, is it?
    Ha. He looked.
ARNO: Your son, the King of Scotland –
MARY: The King of Scotland, ha, he's a naked thing,
    he is this long, I held him in these arms,
    these useless arms, I held him to the moonlight.
    My son. My son? My son.
    May as well call the sun itself my offspring,
    so little does it care, and from so far
    away it glares at me!
ARNO: They poisoned him
    against you long ago. You must forget him.
MARY: I must forget him? Oh, there speaks the voice
    of the wise bachelor. Do you have a mother?
ARNO: I do indeed.
MARY: You're standing in her kingdom.
    Treat it well. Treat *her* well. And when
    she turns her back a moment, make a treaty.
    My sister, my dear sister. It's not her.
    It's Walsingham. My son has not the sense
    to see what's being done. He thinks it means
    some influence with her. No, darling boy,
    it turns you to a puppet. Pocket money.
    He's found a mother better to his liking.
    We all should pick and choose. I can't endure this.

What are you looking at? Are you by a grave,
are you reading what it says, are you translating
epitaphs for children you don't have?
ARNO: I'm looking at the rightful Queen of England.
    I'm looking at her royal silk.
MARY: Royal shroud.
    My son has found a mother. Now the moon
    will shut her eye, for even she can't see
    a point to my remaining. Here's a son,   (*The letter.*)
    here's one who moves for me, beside my heart,
    still biding here, attentive to a mother's
    wish.
ARNO: Let it remain there, I implore you.
MARY: What's your suggested course then, Monsieur Arno,
    another twenty years of you and I
    groping for the one pen in our prison?
    What is it you like about existing
    in this woebegotten hovel with that guard dog
    strutting by? Is it my company?
    Has it escaped your secretarial eyeballs
    that I have been enslaved here? Is it lost
    on your diplomatic nostril that this house
    is neighbour to a sewer? Do you truly
    think nobody knew that when they chose it?
ARNO: I suffer the discomfort at your side,
    but that plan is all impulse –
MARY: Well, a pulse
    may be what's lacking in what's left of us.
ARNO: I only say we need more information.
MARY: Tell the sun, Claude, stop it in its tracks.
ARNO: Your letter may to you be a love token,
    ribboned and, and, perfumed, but it ties you
    to an assassination.
MARY: No it doesn't.
    It's Anthony's design, they are young men,
    they have their dreams, they used to serve me wine.
    It's neither my idea nor my intention,
    but this provides for my deliverance,

or will you build a wall around my every
wish?

ARNO: Yes, where the wolves are!

(*PAULET comes.*)

PAULET: You'll pardon me for an omitted duty
concerning that.

ARNO: Concerning what?

PAULET: That cloth.

ARNO: That is my lady's Royal Cloth of State,
Sir Amyas, it's hung there for eighteen years,
since she first came to England.

PAULET: I do know that,
Mr Secretary.

ARNO: Does it hurt you somehow?

PAULET: Indeed it does.

MARY: I see into the future.

PAULET: It signifies a status that's become
an insult to the throne. These Roman words
are of themselves illegal. Do we speak
Roman in this country?

ARNO: It's in French.

En ma fin, ma commencement.

PAULET: It's not English.

MARY: No, but it's made in England. Is the lacework
tormenting you there, Amyas?

PAULET: The sight of it
is sickening. It was remiss of me
to have allowed it.

MARY: Well. I pardon you.

PAULET: I ask no pardon of a heretic.

MARY: It's freely granted, though. You can't escape it.

PAULET: Do you not comprehend how you're perceived
beyond these walls? Do you have no idea
what kind of threat you are?

MARY: What kind of threat?
But the threat is made of thread, and the thread's made
of nothing you can't break.

ARNO: You have no right
to take it down!

41

PAULET: It has no right to be there.
    And you, in England, have no rights at all.
    (*PAULET goes.*)
ARNO: I shall protest to the Ambassador.
MARY: Oh, rage on legal grounds against the winter
    for all the good it does. I'm now as calm
    as ice that has claimed lives. All is quiet.
    A time has come.
ARNO: I know you. I serve you.
    I love you, as a servant, as a subject,
    I do, and for those reasons once again
    I beg you not to part with your reply
    before we have / received –
MARY: / You're looking at a sun
    that is about to set. It may be sad,
    it may be beautiful, but it will set,
    and what you feel about it is for you, Claude,
    to take with you. I'm going to give my answer
    to the shadow-man.
ARNO: My lady –
MARY: Speak in Welsh,
    then all your lamentations will be soothing.
ARNO: I don't believe I trust him.
MARY: You don't like him.
    That's different.
ARNO: I have an instinct –
MARY: Oh,
    you have an instinct. Well, all I can see
    is that he's risked his life to beat a path
    from here to all my hopes. What have you risked,
    for all your good advice? I may not like him
    either, and I have to like you, Claude,
    since we were wound together, but this isn't
    kiss-behind-the-hedge. See how I'm calm,
    my mind is quite established.
ARNO: For your life
    I would lay down –
MARY: Lay down and sleep then, Claude,

dear, my life is passing from your hands
into my hands.

ARNO: Don't do this.

MARY: And the hands
of gallant gentlemen.

ARNO: The kind of men
who your whole life have cost you everything!

MARY: My. Is that opinion in the memoir?

ARNO: Forgive me.

MARY: Give this letter to the beer-man.
Not because I trust him or believe him,
or like him – how can I not like his courage?
But because I can't grow any more. I need
these walls to disappear. Take it, take it.
Copy out my heart in your best hand.
Copy it, Claude. All your inclinations
can disappear in duty. Go. Say nothing.
Tell him to tell Anthony –
we are all bound together in my prayers.
(*ARNO goes. Darkness.*)

Act Three

(Rain. WALSINGHAM reading the letter.)

WALSING: 'My very good friend, although it has been long
    since I received your letter, the delay
    in this response has been against my will.
    But I hope you realise I am aware
    of the affection you have shown so far
    towards all things concerning me.' All right…
    All right. Arrest her, then.
    (GORGE appears.)
GORGE: Just…arrest her?
WALSING: Yes. This is enough. Isn't it, Thomas?
GORGE: Yes, if you say it is, your grace.
WALSING: You read it.
GORGE: I did indeed.
WALSING: It's indefensible.
    Isn't it?
GORGE: I'm not entirely sure.
WALSING: You're not entirely sure. Why's that, Thomas.
GORGE: I don't know. I just feel – it's a little light.
WALSING: You feel it's a little light? A little light.
    Sir Thomas Gorge is of the frank opinion…
    You're very good. It *is* a little light.
    Do you know what's missing?
GORGE: No, your grace, I don't,
    I thought, perhaps, you'd know.
WALSING: Of course I know.
    It's a little light on detail. Isn't it?
GORGE: Yes, she doesn't strike me as a lady
    all that much concerned with detail.
WALSING: Oh?
    I don't agree. Look. Here she is, suggesting,
    here, the section marked, three different ways
    she might be sprung. She's spoiling them for choice.
    Of course you know her better.

GORGE: Oh no,
   not at all.
WALSING: I've never met the lady.
   I've never had that pleasure. Was it a pleasure?
GORGE: Your grace, it was just a duty –
WALSING: Was it a pleasure?
   You met the queen of everything she thinks of.
   Is she a beauty?
GORGE: Yes.
WALSING: That's better. Fair?
GORGE: Reddish brown.
WALSING: Good conversation?
GORGE: Yes.
WALSING: Good legal brain?
GORGE: Not really.
WALSING: French accent?
GORGE: A *soupçon.*
WALSING: A *soupçon?* Would you fuck her?
GORGE: She's – a queen.
WALSING: She isn't.
GORGE: No – she isn't,
   but no, the answer's no.
WALSING: Fucking liar.
   Where's that file I had… How bad is it,
   the Stafford house, does it stink?
GORGE: That one's a yes.
WALSING:
   We have to move her. Do you know this house?   (*Folder.*)
   There's going to be a trial.
GORGE: Chartley Manor.
   No…
WALSING: Or at the Tower. Or maybe this one.
   Fotheringhay. *You* arrest her, Thomas.
GORGE: Me? Why me?
WALSING: She knows you. It's helpful.
GORGE: She trusts me, we could use that –
WALSING: We could what,
   disguise you as her chambermaid? Good God.

45

She's going to be invited to a hunt.
She will go riding, with her *entourage.*
However...what's his name, I had a list –
GORGE: Claude Arno.
WALSING: Him, separate him from her,
permanently. Bring him down to London.
Make him think he's drunk his last *vin rouge.*
Then go and get the lady.
GORGE: While she's riding?
WALSING: Yes. She'll think she's going on a fox hunt.
She'll also think her friends are on their way.
You'll ride up with some men of mine, she'll see you
galloping, she'll think – *c'est liberation!*
Then anything she says, we'll have our staunch
Puritan on hand to witness.
GORGE: Paulet?
WALSING: Yes, Sir Endless Paulet.
GORGE: With respect,
your grace, he's an idiot.
WALSING: Respect to whom,
to him? He is a diamond in disguise.
GORGE: If you say so.
WALSING: Yes. I do, say so,
Thomas, there's no danger, is there, see?
No danger with Sir Endless. He won't find her
beautiful or reddish brown or find her
accent *elegante,* and we won't find him
lovesick on a lane. There is a task
you need a Paulet for. You couldn't do it.
GORGE: What task is it I couldn't do? My grace,
I will do anything.
WALSING: What, to a queen?
GORGE: She's not a queen. What task?
WALSING: She is a queen.
She is the queen of everything she thinks of.
Arrest her conversation, make her red hair
stand on end.
GORGE: Your grace.
(*GORGE goes.*)

WALSING: Tell her *Bonsoir,*
    tell her *je suis le monsieur de la lune.*
    (*WALSINGHAM goes. The rain fades. Birdsong. Music. MARY*
    dressed for riding. PAULET.)

MARY: Was it you who stopped the rain, Amyas? It seemed
    so sudden that I wondered to myself
    did Amyas put a stop to that? One look
    and all the rainclouds fled. You seem the kind
    who would control the weather if required to.

PAULET: There's little I control.

MARY: You control us,
    don't you, Amyas, when you catch us smiling.

PAULET: I doubt if there's an evil in this world
    that's capable of stopping that. You seem,
    madam, oblivious to circumstances.

MARY: I *am* oblivious to circumstances.
    That's very neatly put. Do I look the part?

PAULET: I – have no knowledge, madam.

MARY: Do you not?

PAULET: I have not hunted, or observed a hunt,
    I am quite unaware of what's required.

MARY: You're dressed just so. Perhaps you hunt at night,
    Amyas, when you think you sleep. I've seen you,
    prowling, just in slippers.

PAULET: If you mean
    to joke then you will joke. I'll do my best
    to smile when called upon.

MARY: Well what about me?
    Do I look like a huntress?

PAULET: Madam, I'm sure you do. I need to tell you,
    madam, not to expect too much today.
    It is a brief excursion.

MARY: Is it, Amyas.
    It's still a dream to me.
    A ride through a bright valley.

PAULET: You have, madam, in all these many years,
    through changing times, been, rain or shine, a person
    fair in all your dealings with me. I,
    myself, was weighted with this charge.

MARY: Oh, Amyas,
    I know you never asked to walk with me
    in our grey yard below the sky. The Lord
    drew this circle round us.
PAULET: May the Lord
    part us when He will.
MARY: And not, I hope,
    as enemies, but as his truant children,
    each one sobbing, telling a different story.
PAULET: Well. You are light-hearted. It's for me
    to carry the burden. I'll see to the horses.
MARY: The strongest, Amyas, and we'll ride together!
    We'll seem like lord and lady to the squirrels!
    (*PAULET goes. MARY is left alone. GORGE appears, coughs.*)
MARY: This isn't a time to be here.
GORGE: No, I'm here,
    your majesty, to say, and now the words
    are lodging in my throat,
    to say I won't be here again. My work
    is done.
MARY: I suppose it is. I suppose it is.
GORGE: When you next see me –
MARY: When I next see you,
    you won't be a beer-keg man. You'll be a man
    with land in France forever, and I forever
    in your debt.
GORGE: There are no debts to pay.
    When I next see you –
MARY: When you next see me,
    I won't be a thing of pity. You must go now.
    Meet me in the other world.
GORGE: I swear,
    your majesty, and if, if I am changed,
    remember me before.
MARY: I won't forget you.
    (*ARNO comes.*)
ARNO: Is this negotiation at an end?
    If Paulet sees you, sir, my lady loses

    all her riding, all her privileges,
    and you'll live in an even smaller dungeon.
GORGE: We're finished, Mr Secretary.
MARY: He's leaving,
    Claude, his work is done.
ARNO: I'm sure it is.
    You'll miss him.
MARY: True.
GORGE: Paulet's turning back.
    He's got a horse for you, he's got a beauty.
ARNO: Then let's proceed.
MARY: Oh much more than a beauty!
    Is he for me, you think?
GORGE: Claude, I do need
    one more word with you.
ARNO: My lady's called for.
GORGE: Yes, but you are not. You need to hear this.
MARY: You stay behind and listen, Claude. This man
    has rolled our eighteen years into one month
    and thrown it on the fire. I won't forget it.
    (*MARY goes.*)
ARNO: Well, what is your word.
GORGE: My word, Claude?
ARNO: What is your word with me. Are you courting danger?
    Do you court everything?
GORGE: In English, Claude.
ARNO: That was in English.
GORGE: Was it?
    I don't know any more. She's mounting, look.
    She likes it pretty well. I can lip-read.
ARNO: Can you. Can you cartwheel on a wire?
GORGE: Yes. As it happens.
ARNO: What is your word, sir?
GORGE: They're moving off. She's riding next to Paulet.
    He rides it like a little boy. The horse
    is realising, look, the horse is thinking:
    I'll have some fun with this one.
ARNO: What are you doing?
    Why are you wasting time?

GORGE: Wasting it? I'm killing it, Claude.

    They've gone beneath the ridge. See those men.

ARNO: What men?

GORGE: Those at the door.

ARNO: I have eyes, yes.

GORGE: They're waiting for you, Claude.

ARNO: Why, they're waiting – why? What is your word?

    What do you have to say to me?

GORGE: *Monsieur,*

    nous allons en vacances.

ARNO: What does that mean?

GORGE: Your bloody language, Claude.

ARNO: Where are we going?

GORGE: *A Londres, pour voir la reine.*

ARNO: To London, why to London? With my lady?

GORGE: No, not with my lady. With me.

    With me and twenty blackbirds.

ARNO: Who are you?

GORGE: I'm someone listening closely to your eyes.

    I heard them say: we're going to run away,

    so now my two are saying: No, in fact,

    you're not, because you can't. You can sit down,

    my eyes are adding, if you look. That's right,

    that's the correct translation.

ARNO: *Ah mon Dieu.*

GORGE: *Mon Dieu, mon Dieu,* and *au revoir, madame.*

    The secret letters are as secret now

    as that high lonely cloud, which had been promised

    a rainy sky to hide in.

ARNO: You have killed her.

GORGE: Stow your *sacrez bleu,* nobody's being

    killed, *mon brave.* What people are about

    to be is questioned.

ARNO: Questioned as to what?

GORGE: See, I was questioned then. I told you so.

    Just call me weather vane.

ARNO: I'll call you traitor.

GORGE: Traitor to what? What is this, a kingdom?

This is a little house that stinks to heaven,
Claude, it's not a realm.
ARNO: It is our realm.
It is our Rome, our Paris.
GORGE: I hope your answers
get better nearer London, or else London's
as near to Paris as you'll ever roam,
mon secretaire…
(*MARY, alone, looking into brightness.*)
MARY: Claude? Where is my Claude?
Amyas, where is Claude? You see those riders?
I can see riders, I can see a hundred
gallant riders, that can't be the hunt,
there are no dogs, are there? Amyas, you see them,
we are outnumbered, aren't we? What these riders
want of us must happen, do you see?
Now I can hear them. Why is Claude not with me?
How can he miss this moment? Do you see them,
are they not a gallant company? Can you not
see them turned all golden!
(*Fade light. Darkness. Rain. ARNO imprisoned.
WALSINGHAM's voice.*)
WALSING: When she replied to Babington in writing,
you copied into cipher what she wrote,
exactly in her meaning. Is that true?
ARNO: I can't see where you are. What time is it?
WALSING: It's nearly six.
ARNO: It's six?
WALSING: Is what I said
true or false?
ARNO: It's true. It's true.
WALSING: It's true.
So why have you forgotten writing this?
'I would be glad to know
the names of the six gentlemen selected
for the accomplishment of the design.'
ARNO: I don't – remember writing it.
WALSING: You don't,
do you, you've forgotten it.

ARNO: No –
WALSING: No?
ARNO: I don't believe she wrote it, or, I mean,
    it never passed through me.
WALSING: It never passed through you.
    It's in the letter Babington received,
    in your code.
ARNO: Cannot be. I'd remember.
    It would have been a death, a – suicide,
    to have expressed it in the way you say.
    I would not have agreed. I only copied
    her letter on condition that she promise
    to send it never, till I say so, yes.
    She sent it anyway. *Quand-même.*
WALSING: In English.
ARNO: What time is it?
WALSING: She sent it with those words.
ARNO: Not with those words. I would have never done that.
WALSING: Why don't you do it now? It's nearly six.
    Why don't you write them now?
ARNO: Six of the morning,
    six of the evening?
WALSING: Why don't you write them now,
    so you can get some rest?
ARNO: Get some…rest.
    Is there going to be a trial?
WALSING: Why don't you write the words you now remember?
    Here they are. You copy them in longhand,
    and then in the same cipher as the letter,
    next thing you'll have a drink, and a good meal,
    a hot bath. That rest. I'd like a rest.
    I'm jealous, Monsieur Arno. Monsieur Arno?
ARNO: Yes?
WALSING: No one is going to contradict you.
    The men behind these letters are not men.
    Not any more. Young Anthony. The gang.
    If we were lucky enough to have a window,
    that could be demonstrated from this building.

ARNO: I have – done nothing wrong. And I have told you
    things I can remember.
WALSING: Then remember
    your mistress is about to be arraigned
    for plotting the destruction of the Queen.
    Conspiring with these gentlemen to kill her.
ARNO: Impossible.
WALSING: Question. Can you see this?
    It's dark, but can you see it?
ARNO: It's a book.
WALSING: Kind of a book, but not a book that tells
    the past. It tells the future, or it makes
    some futures possible. No? It's a passport.
    In fact it's yours. I had it made for you.
    Excellent binding, Claude Arno, age, birthplace…
    How do you say that word: Loraing?
ARNO: Loraine.
WALSING: Lorang.
ARNO: Loraine.
WALSING: Loraine.
    That's where you want to go? What are you seeing?
    The little *eglise*, the vines… Can you see someone
    stirring the soup? I think I can hear *les enfants*.
    A girl remembers you, at the long table.
    The bells are chiming six, she gives a sigh.
    Don't rush at it, don't swing the lamp ahead,
    you'll smash it and see nothing.
    See what's to hand. I'm going to leave you now.
    In quarter of an hour – what is it now,
    it's close to six – in these next fifteen minutes,
    try to remember everything you wrote.
    The more you can discover in the past,
    the more you may deliver to the future.
    It's in your hand, it's in your writing hand.
    Picture yourself the pivot of a balance.
    One move either way, and the mechanism
    makes its mind up smartly.
    (*WALSINGHAM goes. ARNO stares, and begins to write.*)

Act Four

(MARY among piles of papers. GORGE comes.)

MARY: Not too much to count, for a counting fellow.
    One person, no assistants, no servants.
    No legal counsel. Papers numberless.
    One winter night to make a case enough
    to save my life. One interested observer.
    (Don't stand on them. I need them.)
GORGE: What are these…
    Letters from the Queen.
MARY: The Queen my sister.
    She'll put a stop to this. There's not one letter
    here without a promise. And tomorrow
    she'll see me, she'll admit that.
GORGE: I'm not sure
    she's coming, Madam Stuart.
MARY: You're not… She isn't coming?
GORGE: This Commission
    sits with her full authority.
MARY: This Commission
    sits with no authority at all,
    since I'm an anointed queen. But it's, it's sad
    she isn't, though, to see me here, at last
    to see me, see what thing I am, and maybe
    see what thing I was. Since, my whole story
    lies between the two. But she's not coming,
    you're sure?
GORGE: She's still in London.
    What's this pile?
MARY: In…London. Those are cases.
GORGE: Cases?
MARY: Precedents from chronicles.
    Civil Law. Canonical. English.
    Turk. Whatever law they spin a stick
    and choose to try me under. She's not coming.
GORGE: Who needs a secretary?

MARY: You do.
Remind you when you're loyal or you're lying.
I'm sure it slips your mind.
GORGE: It does. What's this one?
All alone, unclassified.
MARY: A poem.
You were a scholar, weren't you? Count the lines.
Have it to remember me.
GORGE: You mean that?
You mean that?
MARY: Well advise me here, Sir Thomas,
will it help me in my trial? I didn't think so.
Fold it and take it home.
GORGE: A queen's hand. I'm – speechless.
MARY: New world for you, I'm sure. It's not my hand,
it's just my heart. My secretary wrote that.
GORGE: Claude, our mutual friend.
MARY: Well. Have you seen him?
GORGE: Claude? Yes, he's well.
MARY: I'm thinking of him.
Let him know.
GORGE: He knows. He thinks of you.
Speaks highly of you, fairly, truthfully.
You know, a legal man, a friend of mine,
agrees you can't be tried.
MARY: O, *merci*, Thomas,
I hadn't thought of that. I'm overwhelmed,
I jump for joy! Of course I can't be tried.
GORGE: I mean, I think the government knows that.
MARY: That's very kind of you. Have you forgotten
where you stand again?
GORGE: You will prevail.
MARY: I will prevail. So, will you jump for joy
when I prevail?
GORGE: I stand before a queen.
I do know that. Whatever crimes are proved,
justly or otherwise, I do know that.
MARY: Well. I thank you. Why don't you write a sonnet?

Why not tell fourteen lies and then go hunting,

like a gentleman. I've half a night to do this.

GORGE: Look, my lady…

MARY: Where? Did you smell your quarry?

Are you hunting for the beer-fox?

GORGE: Look. They sent me here…

MARY: They sent *me* here.

Were you a princess once, and did your sister

lock you in a cave?

GORGE: They sent me here

to oversee – it saddens me in ways

that make no sense –

MARY: Say it, you'll feel better.

GORGE: The confiscation of your private papers.

The confiscation of…all that you have here.

I wish –

MARY: Don't make a wish.

GORGE: I wish –

MARY: Don't make a wish.

There are no wishes left. Somebody drank them.

GORGE: I cannot bear / to be –

MARY: / I cannot bear to hear

how sad you are, Sir Thomas.

I am on trial tomorrow, for my life.

GORGE: Absolutely not –

MARY: You know I am.

In front of fifty judges.

(*GORGE begins to gather the papers.*)

GORGE: They are not

judges, they are counsels, it's a hearing.

You have no case to answer, you're a queen.

MARY: I am a woman trying not to cry.

And you are my last subject, on your knees,

taking the ground away.

(*MARY goes. GORGE gathers the papers and goes in the other
direction. Rain. WALSINGHAM, seated. PAULET.*)

WALSING: Sit, Sir Amyas Paulet. How was your journey?

PAULET: Unusual, your grace. I could not pass

a mile along the road without encountering
ministers of state on their way north.
WALSING: Yes, I'm the last to leave. The French could land
and find no government, unless they tried
to subjugate Northamptonshire. There's a problem.
PAULET: A problem? How, your grace?
WALSING: I've been surprised.
I had been sure your conduct as regards
our Madam Stuart had met with high approval
in the only place it matters.
PAULET: In the only – has it not?
WALSING: I'm as amazed
as you're about to be.
She spoke of you today.
PAULET: Her Majesty?
WALSING: She spoke of the great danger we believe
she is exposed to now. We may have foiled
one plot, but we can see the skin of England's
crawling with our enemies.
PAULET: Indeed,
but the woman goes on trial tomorrow.
WALSING: True,
she does. Let me be brief. Her Majesty
remarks in you a want of diligence.
PAULET: A want of diligence?
WALSING: A lack of zeal.
Yes, you. I was dumbfounded, as you are.
In that you have not yet, these are her words,
'discovered by yourself, without prompting,
a way of putting Madam Stuart to death.'
Any…observations? Take your time.
PAULET: She goes on trial tomorrow. If she's guilty,
the law will – run its course.
WALSING: Of course she's guilty.
We know she's guilty, that may take a morning.
But then Her Majesty, I'll bet my land,
will change her mind nine times before it's over.
Madam Stuart must not, whatever happens,
make it to the scaffold.

PAULET: But the law,
  God's law –

WALSING: I have been quoting words to you,
  Paulet, from your Sovereign, who derives
  authority from God. You are her subject.
  This is her will. You are the agent of it.

PAULET: I – see. It is, indeed, it is, her will.
  I shall, of course – my duty to my sovereign –
  but the Great Commission must first find her guilty.
  It has been said that the legality
  is doubtful –

WALSING: Has it really.
  This is the royal seal, Sir Amyas Paulet.
  This is addressed to me. Why don't you touch it,
  why don't you hold the sceptre in your hands...

PAULET: (*Reads.*) 'Upon the examination of the cause,
  you shall by verdict find the Queen of Scotland
  guilty of the crime
  with which she does stand charged. Accordingly,
  you will proceed to sentence against her.'

WALSING: 'The legality is doubtful...' Not too much
  doubtful there, do you agree, Sir Amyas?
  Ride back to Fotheringhay. When you dismount,
  tell them I'm right behind you.
  (*PAULET goes. WALSINGHAM goes. Rain. Music. MARY*
  writing. As she reads, the COMMISSIONERS start to appear:
  BROMLEY, HATTON, CECIL and WALSINGHAM.
  The Trial. MARY sits, then looks around.)

MARY: So many counsels, and not one for me.

BROMLEY: The Most High and Mighty Queen Elizabeth,
  being not without great grief of mind
  that you would plot destruction of herself,
  her realm, and the subversion of religion,
  has out of her high office and royal duty
  appointed these Commissioners to hear
  the matters charged / against you –

MARY: / But I am not her subject.

CECIL: You'll have time
          / to speak –
MARY: / I am an anointed queen. Only my peers
     can try me. Are you kings yourselves? She knows that.
     You know it too.
CECIL: In crimes as grave as these
     royalty itself forfeits exemption.
MARY: Is that a law you've made?
BROMLEY: And to this end,
     she has appointed men upright and prudent,
     to judge the evidence forthwith presented.
CECIL: For should you clear yourself, we shall rejoice
     at the honour to your name, and the great comfort
     / to the Queen, and to the realm.
MARY: / And if I clear myself, while you're rejoicing,
     who's going to recompense my nineteen years?
     I came here, under promise of assistance,
     of help against my enemies in Scotland –
CECIL: There is here a procedure –
BROMLEY: We don't acknowledge / that –
MARY: / Queen Elizabeth
     made promises of help, which I could prove
     if I still had my papers. I fled here,
     my realm in flames, my royal person threatened,
     and ever since have been held here a captive,
     under no law that's ever been explained.
     Perhaps, as you / yourselves –
BROMLEY: / No aid was ever promised.
     Your protest is in vain, and prejudicial
     to the laws and to the Queen is therefore
     not admitted here.
HATTON: It is not admitted.
MARY: My protest that the law is prejudicial
     to me is prejudicial to the law?
CECIL: Neither captivity nor royal status
     exempt you from this trial.
HATTON: You can be tried
          in absence.

MARY: Absence? Well,
    I am nineteen years / in absence!
BROMLEY: / The Act of Association
    of 1585 establishes
    the right to trial on charges of conspiracy
    any personage on whose behalf
    conspiracy was made.
MARY: You know as well as I
    this law was made expressly for the purpose
    of sending me to death.
CECIL: / Please calm yourself.
HATTON: / An act of treason
    does not require new laws.
MARY: What are the old ones?
    By whose are you proceeding?
HATTON: Ancient laws,
    which show multiple precedents –
MARY: Let's hear them.
    Precedents for trial of a sovereign
    by subjects of a foreign country, please,
    list them, sir.
CECIL: Extraordinary.
HATTON: The most,
    well, there are a number of citations –
MARY: Multiple, let's hear them.
HATTON: The most recent
    relates to Prince Conrad of Hohenstaufen,
    who was both tried and / executed –
MARY: / This is the most recent?
    1162 he died. I'm scarcely
    done with mourning him! And that Prince Conrad
    was captured on the battlefield. I wasn't.
    In any case, the cus/toms of Anjou –
BROMLEY: / I don't believe
    that these minutiae of history
    ought to detain us. Common English law
    is the basis of this sessions.
MARY: Then you have to
    cite me precedent from English law.

Do you not know that?
You make law at your pleasure in this kingdom,
but I am not your subject.
HATTON: Scottish princes
can be by numerous precedents regarded
as owing a feudal loyalty to English.
As recently as King Henry VIII,
for instance, we / can show
MARY: / I should do grave offence
against my ancestors the Kings of Scotland
even to waste my breath. I'm not your subject,
and to the judgment of adversaries
whose minds were made up long ago, I won't
submit myself.
CECIL: Yet you have claimed this throne.
If you are the Queen's heir, you are her subject.
MARY: Has she acknowledged me as heir? Not so.
I do not recognise your right to try me.
I came here to refute the single slander
that I made plots against my sister's life,
a slander quite repugnant to me.
CECIL: Your protest is recorded. Let's proceed.
BROMLEY: Letter from Sir Anthony Babington:
'Myself in person, with ten gentlemen,
and a hundred others of our company,
will undertake the glorious deliverance
or your Royal Person from your enemies.'
MARY: Well? What is this letter?
BROMLEY: You do know it.
It was sent to you by Babington.
MARY: Who's he?
Who is this Babington?
He may have written this, he may have said so,
but I have not set eyes on it. Or you think
I would preserve a letter such as that?
Then this must be a copy. So. You have
no witness and no letter and no proof
he sent it or I got it or I know him.

You're lawyers, I was told. Would you not laugh
if you were taxed with evidence so threadbare?
There are, out in the world,
those who would rescue me, deliver me,
make me Queen of Spain, but it is not
in my hands to help or hin/der them –
BROMLEY: / Your hands
replied to them, however. If I may.
Letter to Anthony Babington, sixth extract:
'My very good friend...I am aware
of the affection you have shown so far
towards all things concerning me...'
HATTON: Oh it seems
she knew him *then!*
MARY: Is this in my own hand?
BROMLEY: It's a transcription.
MARY: Well. Another copy.
Do you have anything in my own hand?
BROMLEY: Tenth extract!
MARY: Tenth extract. This is nonsense.
BROMLEY: 'Orders must be given that as soon
as the gentlemen accomplish their design,
I can be straight delivered out of here.'
There follow three suggested plans of action.
MARY: I never wrote that letter.
HATTON: Can you prove it?
MARY: If I had not been stripped of all my papers,
yes. If I had counsel, in a second.
If I'd been given more than a half-day
to know I faced ordeal in the glow
of all the legal brains in England, well,
who knows what I could prove – that I'm a man?
I sought to win my liberty. I yearned
for freedom, is that natural in England?
Do you think I harbour hopes of regal power?
This withered branch? These twigs?
BROMLEY: Twentieth extract: 'I would be glad to know
the names of the six gentlemen selected
for the accomplishment of the design.'

MARY: What, show me that, that last part, that extract.
    I didn't write – it's not…this is a dream.

CECIL: Babington confirmed that he received this.

MARY: This is a dream, he what?

HATTON: Babington confirmed that he received it.

MARY: Let him confirm it here. I – one accused
    of treason has the right to face the Crown's
    witnesses. You made that law yourselves,
    correct me if I'm wrong.

BROMLEY: Once more a raft
    of tricks and technicalities.

MARY: This letter…
    I mean, this is a dream, I need a moment…
    I didn't write this. Any of it, this –
    this is the work of Walsingham, a man
    I have been warned devotes his waking hours
    to plot how I might die, why does he do that,
    because of the faith I bear.

WALSING: That's curious,
    the notion that one might be put to death
    because of one's religion. Insofar
    as I'm aware, no law-abiding subject
    was ever put to death for his religion,
    not in England.

MARY: I have heard, and read,
    otherwise.

WALSING: For treason, arguably.

CECIL: It is, I feel, an unfair disadvantage
    with which the lady struggles. This indeed
    is that Sir Francis Walsingham on whom
    she speculates so freely.

MARY: You are Walsingham?

WALSING: I can at least rise up in his defence.
    I call God to record that my own conscience
    is clear of any malice or design.
    I admit that, being careful for the safety
    of both my Queen and country, I have keenly
    searched out practices against the same.

MARY: Well. I'm satisfied. That I spoke freely
 of what I heard – I, pray you won't be angry.
 I will in future doubt such accusations,
 and hope you'll be as doubtful for my sake,
 when I am slandered too.
HATTON: Where's the slander?
 These letters are attested under oath!
BROMLEY: It is the testimony / of –
MARY: / Under oath?
 Under torture.
BROMLEY: It is the testimony
 of your own French secretary, Arno,
 that you did correspond –
MARY: Well, Monsieur Arno…
 He was recommended by the Cardinal,
 which meant, he always…Monsieur Arno always…
CECIL: Are you able to continue?
MARY: I'll drink my water, and I'll cross the desert…
 I meant…his loyalty was not, perhaps
 entirely clear. I mean, not always clear
 for whom he was most careful.
 Where is he now? His evidence would straight
 exonerate me.
BROMLEY: Both Babington and Arno,
 without constraint, have testified that you
 both wrote to and were written to not once
 but frequently by / Babington –
MARY: / Well, why aren't they here?
 What does it say about your evidence
 that you won't bring them forward?
HATTON: Once again
 an alien lectures us on English law.
CECIL: They were accounted dangerous to the state.
MARY: Dangerous to the state? They are not here
 because their evidence would clear me –
HATTON: Lies,
 she's guilty, she can't answer!
MARY: Where is Arno?

WALSING: He's made his deposition. It's for you
    to answer what is charged.
MARY: Not one man here,
    were he the brightest advocate in England,
    would have a hope of mounting a defence
    in my position.
HATTON: She admits perhaps
    her position's indefensible!
BROMLEY: At last!
MARY: They have accused me under threat of torture.
    I never met this Babington! I never
    wrote to him!
WALSING: You wrote to him.
BROMLEY: What's this then?   (*The letter.*)
MARY: I never heard of the six gentlemen
    and their design, and trying to prove I did
    is futile. You are lawyers, yet you come
    with copies, with, with hearsay. Monsieur Arno,
    I would not slander him, but I see plainly
    he's saved himself.
WALSING: But he co-operated
    frankly and in full.
MARY: You cannot try me.
    I'm not your subject. Only Elizabeth
    can judge me, and her mind is, is, is foxed
    with rumours of your making.
CECIL: Let's proceed
    now to the question of the English throne.
MARY: Why? What's that to do with what's just gone?
    How can I follow this?
CECIL: When you first married
    in 1558, the French dauphin,
    you bore the royal arms of England, which
    is tantamount to claiming precedence
    over the ruling sovereign.
MARY: I was sixteen,
    sir, I was obliged to by the King
    my new father –
HATTON: You never ratified

the Treaty of Edinburgh, whereby your claims
would be abandoned. When –

MARY: Let me answer that –

WALSING: You're in communication with the thrones
of France and Spain and with the Papacy.

MARY: You, Sir Francis Walsingham, have not
the right to know what passes between princes.

WALSING: When do I have the right? When the fleet of Spain
is rounding Kent?

BROMLEY: They pray for you in Rome
as Queen of England!

MARY: I am a Catholic!
It's not for me to tell His Holiness
what or whom to pray for –

BROMLEY: 'His Holiness'?

HATTON: Do we have the right to say that?

MARY: Let me answer!

BROMLEY: The Queen of England!

HATTON: Only if we're Scots,
then we have!

CECIL: The schemes of Babington
follow upon a host of such attempts,
either to free you, or –

MARY: I am a captive!
How can I stop attempts? I send them money,
the Catholics. This country sends such money
to my own son in Scotland, my own son,
it doesn't make it any fault of England's
should he in some way disobey –
I never wrote those letters. You can't try me.
I am a queen. They are this man's inventions,
to ruin me, to kill me – you are all
my enemies – you are all…

CECIL: I, for one, am indeed an enemy
to the enemies of the Queen.
(*Silence.*)

MARY: What justice, what justice…
I am weak, I am unwell.

I'm alone, in a strange country, where I came
for shelter long ago.
And I had to learn your language, and your laws,
your history. I have never lived a day
at liberty among you. You are all,
this morning, gathered here in rows, you are all
I've ever seen of your society.
My papers have been taken, and there seems
to be no man in England qualified
or brave enough to help me. I wrote letters,
I freely own I sought deliverance
from nineteen years...but these letters here,
picked out, perverted from originals
you can't obtain, attested by strange persons
you can't produce or won't produce...
With scorn and slander you, you mock my faith,
the sacred character I bear as Queen –
This thing you charge me with is a concoction.
I never sought to harm – look at this, look.
This ring I wear came from your royal mistress
when I arrived in England, as a pledge
of friendship and protection. Can you see it?
Remember it. It was upon this pledge
I came among you. Nobody knows better
than you how well this pledge has been respected.
If this means nothing then her word means nothing...
And if her word means nothing, on what grounds
are any of you standing?
I did believe legitimately I
was her successor, some day, one day.
The day's long gone, you only have to look.
I have perhaps some little time to live.
Some nights I have, in my captivity,
some nights been well aware that there are those
who mean to take my life from me unseen,
unwitnessed. But I pray God to allow me,
as I can hear that death is in your language,
that death before you all, in English daylight,

in the Holy Roman faith I hold dear.
I burden you with nothing by my faith.
I wished, all I wished,
when I was Queen in Scotland,
was that the safety of my Catholics
might be preserved, yet by an act of law
the very month I disembarked at Leith,
I did protect the practice of religion
as I found it – Protestant, your creed.
Then I was told by one, for what it's worth,
that nowhere in the chronicles he knew of
was such an edict to be found recorded.
Never, when I reigned, did I attempt
to force my faith upon a living soul.
And though we suffer here as Catholics,
daily derided, ridiculed and threatened,
vengeance I never think of, even dream of…
Now they complain, you know, they write to me,
they say they never lived as free as when I –
well, such is the way…
(*Exhausted, she laughs silently.*)

CECIL: Do you wish to say any more?

MARY: I wish to speak before the Queen. I wish
to have an – an – an advocate. And I,
I wish you to – I wish you to remember,
that the theatre of the world is far wider
than this realm of England. Well. Look at your cloaks,
your hats and boots. I see you were quite ready
to leave when I arrived.
You were pretty harsh with me, for I'm not learned
or clever like you are. Well. God preserve me
from having to deal with any of you again.
And may God pardon you, sir,   (*Walsingham.*)
who knows what you know well.
(*MARY goes, slowly, frail.*)

BROMLEY: What did she tell you, Francis?

WALSING: I don't know.
I have no papers, sorry.

(*Laughter as the ice breaks. The COMMISSIONERS relax. Their lines intermingle and become indistinct.*)

CECIL: Queen of the Castle, rather we should call her.

BROMLEY: Queen of the Gallows, maybe.

HATTON: Can you believe the gall of the / woman?

BROMLEY: / Dangerous precedent, I feel, allowing a speech / like that...

HATTON: / Exactly my position...

WALSING: I warned you, Robert, a command performance was what we might / expect.

CECIL: / She reduced us all to silence, no mean achievement.

WALSING: Astonishment, perhaps, at the wanderings / of her mind...

CECIL: / The intemperance of her speech...

WALSING: Perhaps she killed / her husband with a sermon.

CECIL: / A spot of lunch, Francis, away from the / rabble?

WALSING: / Absolutely. Now there's a door that leads straight out of here, but which door is it...

(*The COMMISSIONERS go.*)

Act Five

(Music. Rain. GORGE looking out, ARNO seated.)

GORGE: Doesn't the rain stop anything? The planks
    are gleaming and the carpenters are drenched,
    but still they work. I wonder where she is.
    I bet she can hear the work. I bet Sir Francis
    thought that a fitting touch.

ARNO: She used to say,
    she always says, '*les hommes*
    travaillant pour le mort.'

GORGE: It's my cell, too,
    Claude, you might translate.

ARNO: Always the men
    are working to the death.

GORGE: She used to say that?
    Always the men are working to the death.
    Did she mean me? I'm nobody. She meant
    the ministers of state. She told me once
    I was a pawn, no more. She couldn't blame me.
    This pawn thanks you, I said. You know, in chess.
    She says I'm dangerous when I've a mind
    to move diagonally. We laughed at that.
    Sir Francis called me much the same, except
    I had changed colour and was moving backwards,
    so he took me. Fair enough. He laughed at that.

ARNO: *Toujours les hommes travaillant pour le mort.*

GORGE: You've said enough in English and in French.
    Your speech at the Star Chamber pretty much
    finished off her hopes.

ARNO: I told the truth.

GORGE: Even so.

ARNO: They're giving me a passport.

GORGE: Are they really. Not before they've made you
    watch the show.

ARNO: I will refuse to watch it.

I am a diplomat of France. I have
immunities.

GORGE: You have a comic streak,
Claude, I'd no idea.

ARNO: Sir Francis swear
I can go home.

GORGE: Sir Francis swear? Sir Francis
doesn't believe a word Sir Francis swear.
He has Sir Francis followed. When he turns
there's nobody. I've worked with him. I know him.

ARNO: I work with Sir Francis now! He said he'd give me
a passport, and a cell with many windows.

GORGE: Many windows, all of which will show
a lady you once loved as a dear servant
hacked to death to save the church in England.

ARNO: That's not why this must be.

GORGE: She knew damn well
why this must be, monsieur. She said to me,
to Thomas Gorge, for God's sake, 'It's an honour
to know my fate is to become the lifeblood
of England's church.'

ARNO: Sir Francis did tell me,
he told me you changed colour.

GORGE: Know what I did?
I was the lucky winner of the prize
of telling her she was to be beheaded.
She looked at me as if she'd told me *I* was.
She placed her hand on her own Roman bible
and started praying. Paulet then complained
she was blaspheming, whereupon she asked
why would an oath mean anything if taken
on a bible that meant nothing, not to her.
Well, I agreed. I pulled rank. Well put,
I thought, I thought it dignified. Next day,
I'm in a cart to prison. *I* change colour?
I always was this swirl of stuff. But you,
she trusted you.

ARNO: She used me. Sir Francis
he told me all these things.

GORGE: And that poor lady
   told me she forgave you. Do you hear me?
ARNO: Sir Francis has forgiven me.
GORGE: Fuck you.
   They didn't even touch you. The word passport
   and you curl up like a cat. When she appears,
   I'll wave my arms so she can see her loyal
   captives in their cell. Perhaps she'll learn
   a last truth about love.
ARNO: She has no love…
   She has no love for servants…
GORGE: Are you crying?
   Are you laughing? Do you know? Do you remember
   knowing what you felt?
   (*PAULET appears. He ignores them.*)
GORGE: So. The jailer jailed. What was your kindness?
   Smell a rose by accident, Sir Amyas?
   Man's run out of noise.
ARNO: They say I'll never
   see my home again! They keep me waking
   all the night, I'll never see my country!
   I was a loyal servant, but she made me
   write, she made me write and it was treason!
   I was a loyal servant, and I loved her
   as a servant, as I told Sir Francis…
GORGE: Claude, *comme çi comme ça.* It's over now.
   We've finished serving her, God only knows.
ARNO: That man. There. He treats her like a slave.
   I always think he treats her like a slave.
GORGE: Him? I know. There's nothing like a slave
   for making miseries of them below.
ARNO: He sent our friends away. He made her walk
   accompanied, he shouted at her always,
   he made her cry! He took her tapestries
   she made with her own hands and tore them up.
   Why did you do that, sir? You are in jail,
   I am in jail, we are all in jail in England,
   sir, we are all the same!
   (*GORGE and ARNO menace PAULET.*)

GORGE: No we're not the same,
    Claude, we are not the same, by which I mean
    we did good deeds at times by Mary Stuart,
    we tried to smooth her path, but every day
    this sheep dog snarled and herded her, this grim
    refuser, this revoker made her life
    unbearable.
ARNO: She said he would have killed her,
    he would have killed her, him, he thinks his God
    is marching in his step, he thinks all God
    is with him in his mind.
GORGE: Hey, Puritan,
    is boxing of the ears to be illegal
    in the New Jerusalem?
ARNO: Is splitting heads?
GORGE: What about his eyes? You think you'll see
    the lady killed? I don't believe these eyes
    deserve what they desire.
PAULET: Your hands off me!
    (*PAULET throws them back.*)
    These eyes won't see the lady killed, that sight
    was seen eight days ago.
    You live in an abandoned world, where fools
    still hold some hope of pardon. Everything
    she had went to the pyre I lit myself.
    I was preparing to depart for home
    when they arrested me.
ARNO: Now my lady's gone.
GORGE: You liar. We were brought here to be shown
    the execution.
PAULET: You? Who are you?
    This man's of no more use. He said the words
    he was required to say, and who are you?
    Many spoke with her in her last weeks.
    Some were kind, some were cruel, some
    are in the Tower and some are free. Myself,
    I tried to do my duty. Her last words
    to any man were said to me.

GORGE: Oh really.
   What, did she thank you kindly?
PAULET: No. She said
   she'd trouble me no more.
ARNO: That was my lady…
   I hear her.
GORGE: Dry your eyes, *mon secrétaire*.
   I don't believe a word. Why are you here?
ARNO: Did she, did she say anything?
PAULET: She spoke
   at length, claiming her innocence in English,
   at length in Roman prayer till it was finished.
   You don't believe me. When she knelt to die
   and was divested gently, she observed
   that she was unaccustomed to assistance
   from men in this regard. Of deepest crimson
   were her undergarments.
GORGE: My, you were close by.
ARNO: *Helas, la reine est morte…*
PAULET: It seems the dog
   can hear his lady's voice.
   (*ARNO weeps. GORGE looks out again.*)
GORGE: Well. What's that out there?
PAULET: I've no idea.
   Somebody's done something wrong.
GORGE: It seems so.
PAULET: A stage is being set.
GORGE: How many men
   are held here in this jail?
PAULET: It's not a jail.
   These warehouses belong to Walsingham.
   We dwell in the one chamber that's in use.
GORGE: Really. What did you do? Why are you here?
PAULET: What did I do? My duty.
GORGE: No, you must have
   disobeyed, or something –
PAULET: I obeyed
   my conscience.

ARNO: She is dead, I can go free,
 I told the truth –
GORGE: Perhaps it's set for him,
 he wrote the letters, didn't he, he knew
 about the murder plot, and he did nothing!
 What did *I* do? Showed a human side.
PAULET: Maybe they're going to hang your other side.
GORGE: You must have disobeyed.
ARNO: *Il y a quelqu'un!*
 Someone is coming now!
GORGE: It's as you say,
 some were cruel and some were kind, I favoured
 kindness but it's not as if I didn't
 help to spring the trap – you think it's easy,
 lying through your eyes?
PAULET: No, I do not.
 It's quite beyond my capabilities.
GORGE: It's Claude, he wrote the words.
PAULET: And testified
 before the Queen of England that the woman
 forced him to, which was believed.
ARNO: She did,
 she did, she looked my way, *la reine anglaise!*
 I'm going to have a passport!
GORGE: Yes for sure,
 you're heading for a hotter realm than this one.
ARNO: I have been promised!
GORGE: I've done nothing wrong!
ARNO: You lied to my poor lady!
GORGE: And you killed her!
 (*ARNO and GORGE fight, then sit back, exhausted.*)
GORGE: If…if it is me. I want it known,
 my job was to deceive her, which I did
 for the protection of the English throne.
 My actions afterward, what some may term
 kindness, were a duty too, a duty
 to a still, inner, sense of what's, what's right,
 what's Christian. That's all.

75

ARNO: I loved her, and in love, in a servant's love,
    I did what she command. I did insist
    she never send the letter, but she send it.
    If it is me they come for, I would like
    this is recorded to her son in Scotland.
    And that his mother always thought he loved her.
PAULET: There's nothing I can say to you the world
    can't see before its eyes. That I did serve
    loyally my Queen and the Good Lord,
    and where I fell was where the pathways forked,
    and it was lonely on the one I chose.
GORGE: I'll say that for you, Amyas.
PAULET: Then I'm grateful.
    I'll do the same for you, and for this phantom,
    unless the stage they build is one of three.
    (*Steps approaching. WALSINGHAM comes.*)
WALSING: You three continue to surprise me. Look.
    It opens from inside. I told the warder
    to see how long you'd sit in here without
    attempting an escape. Have you knotted sheets?
    Have you dug holes? Not ostentatious holes.
    Subtle holes? My kind? And all the time
    you never tried the door. What does that prove?
    perhaps that you believe
    you are where you belong.
GORGE: Sir Francis, we
    do all admit our weaknesses, and do
    most solemnly repent them –
WALSING: Weaknesses?
    You can repent a sin, you can't repent
    a weakness.
ARNO: Sir, Sir Francis, I have been
    forgiven –
WALSING: Who forgave you?
ARNO: You, Sir Francis.
WALSING: When, in a time of weakness? Is this you?   (*Passport.*)
ARNO: *Merci, mon Dieu, merci!*
WALSING: That's enough mercy.
    (*ARNO goes.*)

GORGE: Sir Francis, I have served you –
WALSING: God defend me
  from service. This is yours.   (*Passport.*)
GORGE: This isn't me.
WALSING: There isn't one for a Sir Thomas Gorge,
  because he's dead, you understand. This man
  is you, and you are going to ride with Claude
  to Dover and depart for southern France,
  where you will serve me further, at arm's length.
  Say nothing, you don't yet know how you sound.
  (*GORGE goes.*)
WALSING: You are alone with God.
PAULET: I always was.
WALSING: Or am I alone with God?
  (*WALSINGHAM contemplates what's outside.*)
  So many carpenters. Not so many virgins.
  No star shining. Nowhere to rest your head.
  Have you a sermon there, Sir Amyas Paulet?
  For you've turned the devil's colour.
PAULET: I call on God to hear me –
  I would not make a shipwreck of my conscience,
  to spill her blood outside the law. The lady
  was justly tried. There is no man alive
  who had the right to take from her the death
  she wanted. I went to her in her room
  and heard her breath and heard my Queen's command,
  but over all heard God in that same breath,
  and I let her be. I disobeyed on earth,
  but have, as I believe, obeyed in heaven.
WALSING: Amyas, you are speaking in a language
  new to me. What blood?
PAULET: I was referring
  to the command –
WALSING: Command,
  what command?
PAULET: It had the royal seal,
  and it commanded me –
WALSING: What royal seal?

PAULET: I thought you showed me –
WALSING: Why would I show *you*
   a document that bore the royal seal?
   Who are you?
PAULET: What, then, am I guilty of?
WALSING: Rack your brains and see if they confess.
   Here we are, it's starting.
PAULET: What's starting?
WALSING: What's starting? Life is starting.
   It's market day. You see they've built a stage
   to sell their livestock. Is that frivolous
   to puritans? Life and its pure bargains?
PAULET: A stage – to sell the livestock.
WALSING: Are you buying?
   You have new lands to farm, as was agreed.
   Bid on something that can get you home.
   Tell them you're with me.
   (*PAULET goes to the door, uncertain, and then out.*)
   Tell them we're together.
   (*WALSINGHAM goes. Fade to dark. Rain.*)

WOLFPIT

The Tale of
The Green Children of Suffolk

Nor does it seem proper to pass over a prodigy unheard of by generations which is known to have happened in England under King Stephen. And indeed I have hesitated long over this matter, which was related by many; and the thing seemed to me either of no or of concealed reason, ridiculous to repose faith in; until so overwhelmed by the weight of so many and such witnesses as to be compelled to believe and marvel at what I cannot approach or explain by any forces of the intellect.

There is a village in East Anglia four or five miles distant, it is said, from the noble monastery of the blessed king and martyr Edmund. Near which village are seen certain very ancient pits, which are called in the English tongue 'wlfpittes', that is, the pits of the wolves, and bestow their name upon the village which they adjoin. Out of those pits at the time of harvest, the reapers being busy about the gathering of the fruits throughout the fields, there emerged two children, male and female, green in the whole body and of strange hue, clad in raiment of unknown material. And when they were wandering stunned through the field, they were seized by the reapers and led into the village, and with many tears at the sight of so much that was novel, for several days were tried with offered food. When they were almost dead with fasting, nor attended to any of the foods which were offered to them, by chance some beans happened to be brought from the field; which immediately seizing, they sought the lentil itself in the stalks, and finding nothing in the hollow of the stalks, wept bitterly. Then certain of those who were present offered them the legume plucked out of the shells; which immediately accepting, they ate freely.

They were nourished by this food for several months, until they knew the use of bread. Thereupon, little by little changing their own colour, through the prevailing nature of our foods, and rendered like us, they also learned the use of our language. And it seemed to the wise that they should receive the sacrament of holy baptism, which indeed was done. But the boy, who seemed to be the younger, living a short time after the baptism, was removed by premature death; his sister, however, remaining safe and sound, nor differing in much from the women of our kind. Indeed, she afterwards took a husband at Lynn, it is said, and a few years ago was said to be still living.

When they had the use of our tongue, being asked who and whence they were, they are stated to have replied: 'We are people of the land of Saint Martin, who undoubtedly is held in especial veneration in the land of our birth.' Subsequently asked where that land might be, and by what means they had come from thence, they said: 'We know neither. This much we remember: that when one day we were grazing our father's cattle in a field, we heard a certain great sound, as we are now accustomed to hear at St Edmunds, when they are said to sound the tocsin. And when we heard that sound which we wondered at in our souls, suddenly, as if fallen into some departure of the mind, we found ourselves among you in the field where you were reaping.'

Asked whether in that place there was belief in Christ, or whether the sun rose, they said that land to be Christian and to have churches. 'But the sun,' they said, 'does not rise in our native places; its rays illumine our land very slightly, restricted to a measure of that brightness which among you either precedes the sun in the East or follows it in the West. Moreover, a certain lighted land is seen not far from our land, the two being divided by a very broad stream.' These and many other things, long to unravel, they are reported curiously to have replied to those inquiring, and let what conclusions that can be drawn concerning these matters. I myself am not ashamed to have set forth the prodigious and marvellous event.

William of Newburgh
(c.1136 – c.1198)

A...wondrous thing...happened in Suffolk at St Mary Woolpit. A certain boy was discovered with his sister by the inhabitants of that place, lying by the edge of a pit which exists there, who had the same form in all members as the rest of mankind, but in the colour of their skins differed from all mortals of our habitable world. For the whole surface of their skins was tinged with a green colour. Nobody could understand their speech. Being accordingly brought out of wonder to the house of Master Richard Calne, a soldier, at Wicks, they wept inconsolably.

Bread and other food was brought to them, but they would eat no victuals which were placed before them, even while tormented for a long time by the greatest pangs of hunger, because all food of that kind they believed to be inedible, as the girl afterwards avowed. At length, when some beans newly broken off with their stalks were brought into the house, they made signs with the greatest avidity that those beans should be given to them. Which being brought to them, they opened the stalks in place of the bean-pods, thinking the beans to be contained in the hollows of the stalks. This some of those standing by noticed, and opened the pods and showed the naked beans, which being shown they ate with great joy, for a long time touching no other food at all. the boy, however, always as it were oppressed by languor, after a short time died. But the girl, enjoying continual good health, and become used to any kind of food, entirely lost that leek-green colour, and gradually recovered a sanguine habit of the whole body.

She afterwards being regenerated by the holy bath of baptism, and remaining for many years in the service of the aforesaid soldier (as from the soldier and his household we frequently heard), showed herself very lascivious and wanton. Questioned frequently concerning the men of the region, she averred that all dwellers and things in the region were tinged with a green colour, and that they perceived no sun, but enjoyed a certain brightness such as happens after sunset. Questioned further by what means she had come into this land with the aforesaid boy, she replied that because they were following some cattle, they came into a cave. Having entered which, they heard a certain delectable sound of bells, caught up by the sweetness of which sound, they walked for a long time wandering through the cavern, until they came to the exit of it. Whence emerging, as if stunned by the too great brightness of the sun and unaccustomed temperature of the air, they lay long at the edge of the grotto. And when they were terrified by the agitation of those who came upon them, they wished to flee, but could in no wise discover the entrance of the cave, before they were seized by those arrivals.

Ralph of Coggeshall
(d. 1227)

Characters

TOM PARCH

NED STANER

SARA STANER

BETHAN COLEY
villagers of Woolpit

WHITYARD
the village reeve

MASTER RICHARD CALNE
a soldier, the lord of the manor

DEAZIL
a churchman from the Abbey

THE GREEN GIRL

THE GREEN BOY

JUXON
a man from Lynn

The play takes place primarily in the year 1154, in the village of Woolpit, Suffolk, during the civil war between King Stephen and the Empress Matilda. The village is under the jurisdiction of the great Abbey or 'Liberty' of Bury St Edmunds.

This play was first performed in August 1996 at the Garage Theatre, Edinburgh, by the Cambridge University Amateur Dramatic Club, with the following cast:

PARCH, Simon Kane
STANER, Nick Falk
SARA, Gabi Woolf
BETHAN, Jessica Slater
WHITYARD, Henry Paker
CALNE, Jamie Griffith
DEAZIL, Corrin Helliwell
JUXON, Dave Allen
GREEN GIRL, Lucy Muss
GREEN BOY, Jessica Boyde

Director, Sally Moss
Composer, Anthony Sycamore

Wolfpit was workshopped at the National Theatre Studio in September 1993, under the direction of Greg Doran. This version of the play arose from that work.

Act One: Summer

Scene One

The fields at Woolpit. Harvest. Daylight.

SONG

Start where you stop
 Hoist the high hoop
Day, night and crop
 From a skip to a stoop
Jump through the ring
 Day, night, everything
Jump through the ring
 Priest, peasant, king,
Until all pass through
 Then I'll jump through too.

The hawthorn go by,
 Good fortune in May,
The green elderflower
 Jump through, jump through!
Dark elderwood too,
 The Judas tree,
Leap through the hour
 And be memory.

Go by, by St John,
 Herb-Robert in June
And the roses ablaze
 Jump through, jump through!
Wild strawberry too,
 And on Midsummer Night
Leap high through the haze
 And be gone from sight.

Go by, the dry hay,
 Through a yellow July
And the Queen-of-the-Meadow

Jump through, jump through!
The good wormwood too,
At the Dog Day Fair,
Leap and your shadow
Will lose you there.

Go by, the great Harvest,
Go by, golden August,
The corn in the light
Jump through, jump through!
The silverweed too,
Black poppy and beer,
Leap the blue night,
And tomorrow is here.

The fairs of September
Go by, now the summer
Is home from the day
Jump through, jump through!
And the hazelnut too,
And the blackberries in,
Leap clear into May
And my song will begin.

Start where you stop
Hoist the high hoop
Day, night and crop
From a skip to a stoop
Jump through the ring
Day, night, everything
Jump through the ring,
Priest, peasant, king,
Until all pass through,
Then I'll jump through too.

(*Tom PARCH decides to have lunch.*)

PARCH: Let's have no quarrel. God's an elevener,
and opens up His box of lunch when I do.
What does He eat then, Tom? Same as I do,
meat and a leaf or two, 'cause all the time
He's thinking, not unlike I do – we got

this field to reap, we got to reap it, we got
labouring force – that's me and Him – and we got to
keep 'em strong, and what that takes is eating.
Eating, reaping, sleeping, eating, sleeping.
(Think I might have skipped a reaping there
but there's your essence.) Mmm. Meat and a leaf.
Rabbity-thin green stuff. This is what keeps
Ned Staner rabbity-thin, and if I eat too much
I'll gawk about like him, I'll wenge away,
I shall. I shan't. I shan't, I'll keep me strong
with a little refreshening sleep, it says in our Book:
'The sleep of a labouring man is sweet', and it is.
Take that from a labouring man, and a sleeping too,
a man with both those skills.
Mmm… Now, if they see me in the field
they'll say, 'Tom Parch is sleeping! When he wakes
we'll see such labour done, we'll have the harvest
in by dinner, and we'll all thank Tom Parch
and bump him first to the ale-keg!' Here he comes,
old shadow-man in shade of the beech he wedded.
(*Enter STANER, SARA, and BETHAN.*)

STANER: We told the time by you, Tom Parch, a time
for leisure after labour. When we saw you
down the scythe there was among us others
a general downing.

PARCH: You're in the wrong, Ned Staner.
There's labour for the weedy, and there's labour
for the mightiest like me: we need our leisure
oftener than the ordinary.

SARA: Mightiest?
His might is all 'I reckon it might be lunchtime.'

PARCH: Look at all my flock, though, Mrs Staner.
No one came by to listen to our Jesus
except they got a feast for doing nothing.
But even He with a rack of loafs and fishes
could never grow a muscle on your Ned here.

SARA: True enough, he's a frail and idling twig,
but you, Tom, make him seem a toiling Adam.
Don't you reckon, Beth?

BETHAN: Tom makes a dead man
    seem a man of business.
PARCH: Chuckle on,
    you burrow-dwellers, your unmanly frames
    can't do the half of what this can.
SARA: He points
    his muscles out, but he must mean his belly.
STANER: It's true, I never get no share off him,
    he says, 'You should eat more, Ned,' with his gob full.
SARA: He probably don't see you, skinny fool,
    you pass behind a hayrake and go missing.
BETHAN: Had it again there, Sara, sort of a shiver,
    like I said, been shivering all morning.
SARA: Vertigo on account of how you're taller
    than ever you were in the world. No one can cure you.
STANER: The reeve'll cure you, Beth, now here he comes
    processing through the crops.
BETHAN: Don't anyone feel it?
    (*Enter WHITYARD, the reeve, their overseer.*)
WHITYARD: What do you think you people are up to here?
SARA: We think we're reapers and up to about this far.
    We circled then to a school,
    for Master Parch to show us the way with the scythe.
WHITYARD: Parch's way with the scythe
    is prop it against a bale and use the blade
    to hook his luncheon basket. Learn his way
    and we'll give thanks for beanmash in November!
    This is one whole village of afternooners.
    Each of you was given a strip to reap
    from sunrise to sunset.
PARCH: Well we held a dance
    and a song alongside, Master Whityard, it's only
    how we keep our spirits up.
WHITYARD: Are we reaping
    songs this summer? What if it rains? And then?
    Jigs and chuckles in a churn of mud.
PARCH: Rains, rains how, almighty King of the Mowers?
    There's not a cloud, there's not a sleeve of cloud
    to hide the ace of thunder up.

WHITYARD: I've heard
   the frogs outcroaking Father Time, I've heard
   sootfall more than common down my chimney,
   Tom, and swallows flying low and hooded.
PARCH: Well spotted, Master reeve, but it ain't raining.
BETHAN: You feel it too?
WHITYARD: What's that I feel?
SARA: Hot air.
BETHAN: Again I've a shiver, Sara.
STANER: Wolf's in the corn.
WHITYARD: All I know is Harvest time is a time
   for nothing else than harvest, so – hup tools!
   This is Master Parch's strip, from the wolfpit
   to the mark I made there. Then it's yours and Sara's,
   then hers until the brook. Ned, hup tools!
STANER: I'm working along with you, Sara.
SARA: On a field
   in the same one world, if so you mean by 'along'.
   (*Exit SARA, STANER and BETHAN.*)
WHITYARD: Come on, Tom, hup tools!
PARCH: I'm hupping 'em.
   (*Exit WHITYARD. PARCH downs the scythe again.*)
PARCH: But you do know what they say about too much
   work on top of a bite, if it's all abruptish.
   I'll lend some moments to the working up
   a proper plan. Old dad, he always planned.
   'Tom, I have a plan,' I never forget
   his saying that. Last thing he ever said.
   First, before the plan, make sure the others
   are keeping a good old line. Hmm, that's the line,
   all sweating away in the heat of a master plan.
   Nothing quite like work to get that sense
   of all of us together, all as one.
   'There's one event that happeneth to 'em all!'
   That's in the Book. The Book, that's like a plan.
   Ned, speed up a bit there! Keep in the line!
   (*Two GREEN CHILDREN begin to emerge from the pit behind
   him. PARCH is watching the other workers.*)

PARCH: Keep 'em in line, else how shall the corn be in?
    Now why are they looking at me? All you women,
    hup those tools! You're quitting it like children
    when there's an hour to lunch! Or a shade under.
    And now they start to tread my way – you never
    seen a man at work? What have I done?
    I'll touch my head for a halo, sure they walk
    like worshippers of mine, fixing to fall
    toward me and cry, 'Master!'
    Still they come, yet now they up their scythes
    as if to warn or threaten me! Poor Tom,
    with all his deaths approaching at a stroke –
    they tilt the earth, a man could lose his balance!
    (*He sees the CHILDREN and jumps in the pit. Enter SARA,*
    BETHAN and STANER.)

BETHAN: The air is still for shock.

SARA: Jig of the heat.

BETHAN: What do you see?

SARA: Brats rolled in a byre.

BETHAN: Two children, I.

STANER: The eyes are come my way.
    I drank last night.

BETHAN: Well I drank not a drop.

STANER: But they ain't green to your eyes.

BETHAN: Oh they are.
    As leaf, as elderflower.
    What happened to you, dears?

STANER: They can't be there.

BETHAN: They look at us as if
    it's us who can't be. This was the shiver, Sara,
    a voice is saying, an elder voice inside.

SARA: A voice inside is muttering some clot
    has dipped his brood in a pond and then forgot 'em.
    Can't say I blame him.

BETHAN: Children, can you see us?

STANER: They can't see me. They stare but stare right through me.

SARA: No change there.

BETHAN: Changelings, Sara, you reckon?

SARA: No such things as those.

STANER: Nor never was.

BETHAN: Then, apple-children, children of the dell?

SARA: Children dabbed with green to make a fool
     of folk as green as them.

BETHAN: You say they *are* green!

SARA: We say we're pink or white and we ain't either.

BETHAN: I'll touch them with my different kind of hand.

STANER: I wouldn't, you might die of what they got.

SARA: Dye's the word, be dyed with what they ducked in.

BETHAN: What have they got?

STANER: Green, they somehow got,
     and you don't see nothing never
     green round here, except it got no face.

     (*BETHAN reaches out her hand. The CHILDREN panic.*)

GIRL: Agaradee, omoriko, jaghaia!

STANER: Words, they're of our world.

SARA: Of course they are.
     Everything's of our world that's in our world.

BETHAN: Those words weren't of our world.

STANER: They was green words.

BETHAN: So what, so ours are white words, Ned Staner.

STANER: White maybe, but white is what we got.

SARA: Tom Parch, you yellow-belly, where'd you find
     these muddy urchins?

     (*PARCH emerges.*)

PARCH: Yellow, Sara Staner?
     Who had to search the pit for further perils?
     I did, and did. All clear. Don't mention it.

BETHAN: Was there a hole? They must have got through a hole.

SARA: Really, Beth, they wandered along and fell.
     They're stragglers of some fair, some carnival.
     I say we leave 'em.

BETHAN: Them so beautiful.

SARA: Crown 'em King and Queen of Corn, why don't you.

STANER: I say we sling 'em back in the wood they're from.

BETHAN: I say they're sick and we should try to help them,
     Christian like.

STANER: There ain't no green in the Book.
 Parson Deazil said. If he saw them two
 it be over quick, with a rope.
PARCH: You can all belt up.
 I saw them first. I found them on my strip.
 While they stop here, then them's my property,
 green or black or multivarious orange.
SARA: Sure, Tom Parch, no doubt you speak their garbage.
PARCH: That I do. I heard it. On my travels.
STANER: Travels, Tom? I never saw you travel.
PARCH: You wouldn't, would you, clod? When I was with you
 I wasn't on 'em, and, when I wasn't, I was.
SARA: Enough, I say, away, you horrors, leave us!
GIRL: Sannaki, gaghai! Coru, cheruda, coru!
PARCH: It's up to me who can and can't touch whom,
 good people, as the finder.
 (*Enter WHITYARD.*)
WHITYARD: Sky above.
 I do declare these children somewhat green.
SARA: St Peter, so they are. I wish I'd been
 elected reeve at Woolpit.
PARCH: Master Whityard,
 These children have arrived in my domain –
WHITYARD: It's Master Calne's domain.
PARCH: But it's my strip.
 and there they are, arrived.
WHITYARD: They are both children,
 and two in total number.
 Now, children, what's your business in our fields?
GIRL: Domir carukk – calhaiko –
WHITYARD: Lincoln, is it?
BETHAN: Who knows, it could be language
 out of the woodland.
SARA: Anything meaning nothing,
 Beth'll swear to God it's High Goblin.
 This is a trick to stop us in our work.
WHITYARD: Concluding of a close examining,
 I say we take 'em to the Woolpit well

and bathe 'em wholly vigorous, till such time
they look as we do, and can toil as we do,
then –
PARCH: It's a proper plan, but it ain't my plan,
Master King of the Mowers. Now, my plan –
BETHAN: Master Whityard, take 'em to the village
in daylight and – who knows, what with the war –
you'll get some folk see evil everywhere,
would fall upon the children as a sign
of evil coming –
STANER: Greenness *is* a sign
of evil coming, I heard somewhere. In a church.
PARCH: My plan is that you all resume to labour
while I instruct my children in the ancient
customs of old Woolpit.
SARA: Well we know
what Tom'll custom her to.
STANER: Listen, Tom,
I don't like this. I lost my footing here.
I like a day like yesterday, like when
only the old things happen.
BETHAN: Master Whityard,
We got to keep them hidden!
WHITYARD: Concluding of a listening to all points,
I say I should myself stand in a guard
beside the weird intrudants, till such time
as water can be fetched to fully wash 'em.
Sara, Bethan, run to the well at Woolpit
and fill two pails, and bring 'em, on no account
outspilling a word to any about the occurrence.
Which thus concludes my plan.
BETHAN: Sara, let's run.
SARA: Before this trickles off them in the sunshine.
(*Exit BETHAN and SARA.*)
PARCH: I see our fellows wondering, Master reeve,
what's the business. Wave 'em on, I should.
WHITYARD: I'll wave 'em on. Honest work, you fellows!
STANER: I say we take 'em, now the women's gone,

take 'em away, forgetting 'em. You frogs,
we seen through you! We come up with a plan
to make like you were never here!

PARCH: Ned Staner,
we chase 'em off, there's nothing left but labour.
And see how far the sun's off from his sunset.

STANER: No good, they mean, the way they grope about
and talk no word no Christian never spoke.

WHITYARD: Nor wore such cloth, Ned Staner. Look at it,
I do declare it seems to be – we'll scrub 'em.
They'll catch a cold of English and go home.

STANER: I would they would. My home won't be my home
till I forget 'em. Plagues!

WHITYARD: Enough, Ned Staner!
With all they are, it's children that they are.
Here come the women with two water-pails.

STANER: Hear that, plagues? It's pails to make you pale
as I am! Pails to make you pale! You get that?
(*Enter BETHAN and SARA with pails of water.*)

BETHAN: Don't worry, dear, we only want to help you,
we only – Sara, feel,
it don't feel like it's mud, it's delicate
and whorled like skin! But it's green, it can't be skin.

PARCH: Of course it's not a skin, it's a green film.
If you won't start with Adam's ale, I'll start
with Parch's spit – come here!

STANER: You'll make him pale!
(*PARCH grabs the BOY, who bites him.*)

PARCH: Damn this dredgling, look! Look what he did!

SARA: That's probably not real blood, that's just a film.

PARCH: See this, boy? That's red, that is, Man red!

STANER: They snort to see our blood! I vote we burn 'em!

SARA: We scrub 'em, we decided. Anyroad,
you burn someone for laughing at Tom Parch,
there's all the kingdom turned into a torch.

WHITYARD: Rinse these children scarlet!

STANER: Harder, harder!

BETHAN: Scrub them any harder,
they'll bleed.

STANER: So bleed.

SARA: I can't scrub any harder.

WHITYARD: By God in Heaven, they're clinging to their colour!
    I swear it's even darkening, like the scum
    of pools when they cloud over.

STANER: Tom Parch,
    you take command, you found 'em. I say drown 'em.

BETHAN: Heaven forbid it!

PARCH: Plainly these are freaks,
    I grant you, but then all points out of Suffolk
    alien things abound.

STANER: It's fever, I said,
    and catchable!

BETHAN: So green is what you are,
    you little loves, you honest elves!

STANER: Tom Parch,
    you put a stop to this, or the world will fill
    with crawling things incurable, and all
    the night I'll itch and tremble.

PARCH: Mere freaks,
    Ned Staner, dry your drivel.

WHITYARD: Hear me now!
    Concluding of the truliness of the greenness,
    I shall approach myself to the manor house
    and ask advice of Master Calne the soldier
    concerning what's to do with what was found.

PARCH: Found by me, that is.

STANER: Don't claim 'em, Tom,
    not now they're green for keeps.

PARCH: (*To STANER.*)   You hush, Ned Staner.
    It's rarities they are. So ask yourself:
    what's good about what's rare. You ask yourself.

STANER: (*To PARCH.*) I'm asking, Tom, I'm waiting on my answer.

PARCH: (*To STANER.*)
    Quit when you have a beard you're tripping over,
    Ned. See how these idiots are gaping?
    That could be all of England congregating,
    Itching for a peek, and I see ourselves
    Passing round a sack, do you see?

STANER: Oh, Tom…

WHITYARD: All you people, four in number, remain
    and guard the weird intrudants, and remember,
    hide them back in the pit if the reapers come.
    I shall inform all others to return
    straightwise to the village at the sundown.
    (*Exit WHITYARD.*)

PARCH: That's what I call labour, standing guard.

BETHAN: Don't worry, children, he'll be back again,
    and when he comes again he'll bring the soldier.

PARCH: The only soldier no one ever told
    we have a war in England.

STANER: We've a war
    but he don't go to it!

SARA: He can fight with me
    any day.

STANER: He wouldn't, he's not a soldier,
    is he, is what Tom's meaning. Fighting a woman!
    My woman's mad!

PARCH: Mad for a bout of warfare.

BETHAN: Hush, don't you see they're frightened? There, there,
    children, you got nothing at all to fear
    at Woolpit village, whoever you are.

SARA: I declare
    April first came once and twice this year.

PARCH: You hush yourself, you ladies. Guardian Tom
    is watching over his children.

SARA: Over his children?
    Somebody else's children.

BETHAN: Our children.

STANER: Never. Nobody's children. Nobody's nothing.
    (*BETHAN, SARA, PARCH and STANER settle down to
    watch them.*)

Scene Two

Calne's house at Wicks. Evening.

(*CALNE, DEAZIL.*)

CALNE: Parson, what would you do in hell? This war
    goes stumbling through the world like a giant child
    happy to set a fire in every field.
    There's not a side to take.
DEAZIL: I'm merely saying
    the policy of the Abbey is distinctly
    shifting from the Empress. As a knight
    of the Liberty it's right that you should know it.
CALNE: So I have the liberty to make a choice?
DEAZIL: Assuredly so, you are assuredly free.
CALNE: Then here I stay, defending what is mine.
DEAZIL: As should we all, Sir Richard. You will inform me
    of any riders strange to you at Woolpit?
    For these must be reported to the Abbey
    without delay.
CALNE: I'll take that liberty.
DEAZIL: That would be best sir. This is a testing time.
    I'm off to Cugford village, where they say
    they saw black riders higher than their black houses.

Scene Three

The Wolfpit. Moonlight.

(*PARCH with STANER; SARA with BETHAN; the
GREEN CHILDREN awake, huddled.*)

STANER: You awake, Tom Parch?
PARCH: That I am,
    though feigning this rolled attitude of sleep
    the best to guard against a creeping up.
STANER: Who's creeping up?
PARCH: Well no one's creeping up.
    Which shows it works. They all think I'm asleep.

STANER: That's good, that is. I'm doing that as well now.
    And no one's creepin' up.
    Tom.
PARCH: Yes, Ned.
STANER: What do you think they are?
PARCH: I don't care what they are, but what I think is:
    I've found a thing I have a mind to keep,
    it being some way rare.
STANER: But you're not thinkin'
    They're ghostly, like, or from this *other place?*
PARCH: You worry what they are, Ned Staner. Me,
    I'll worry what we do with them, they being
    fated to my care.
STANER: I know the answer.
    We should have scrubbed 'em harder, and that's all.
    – You awake, Tom Parch? Now he's asleep.
    It's up to me to guard against creepin' up…

BETHAN: I think the pit's enchanted. Look how they stare!
    The moon's what it is. Maybe the moon's their home!
SARA: Maybe the moon's *my* home, and maybe for that
    I sigh and sicken, it so far away.

STANER: Look, Tom Parch, they're starin' at the moon,
    and Bethan Coley's saying it's like their home!
PARCH: You ought to know, you raked it from your pond
    often enough to look.
STANER: We should of drowned 'em.
PARCH: Now I'm asleep, and thinkin'.
STANER: I'm awake,
    and empty as a barn. I say burn 'em…

BETHAN: Wake up, Sara, she pointed at the moon
    and watched her arm go silver!
SARA: Now she's silver.
    Let's mint her while she sleeps.
BETHAN: I'm doing the same.
    Look, dear, two of us silver, just the same!
    I'm showing I'm just like her.

SARA: That's very kind,
    except you didn't crawl from out a weed farm
    to gather all of Woolpit in a field
    for the amusement of the constellations.
    But see, the joke grew old, they merely wink.
BETHAN: But the moon smiles on them always,
    the moon smiles back at them.
SARA: All of the world
    calls that a smile. I call it a frightened stare
    at something crawling up behind us.
STANER: (*Leaping up and pointing.*)   Riders!
    Barons off of the wars! I'm gone from here!
SARA: It's the soldier, fool, the soldier come to see
    our miseries in threads.
BETHAN: We're over here,
    Master, over here! He's seen us now!
    (*Enter CALNE and WHITYARD.*)
WHITYARD: You see all gathered the four here, Master Calne,
    the four who did the witnessing of the two.
PARCH: And the one who did the finding, Master Calne,
    Thomas Parch here fostering in the darkness.
CALNE: Let's see your little children. Are they brown?
SARA: No, sir, they go whatever shade you care for.
    Bethan likes them silver. Me I'm just
    a lady-hue, I've fallen out of fashion.
BETHAN: Be gentle with them, sir, don't fright them so.
CALNE: Of course. Will you say your name? What's your name, boy?
    – They can't stay here. We're going to have to hide them.
PARCH: You want to take these children off, I have to
    claim a rent, account of how I found 'em.
CALNE: You found a day off work, and there's your rent.
    The crop is in, no thanks to the assembled.
PARCH: (*To STANER.*) Nor him, the knight who spends a civil war
    debating with himself about himself.
CALNE: This girl has a look of wonder. Not the boy, though.
BETHAN: All the words so far has been her words.
CALNE: Oh?
    But not our words?
WHITYARD: *Dream* words is what they were.

CALNE: A lovely face at least in the half-light.

PARCH: She'll disappoint at dawn, like a true wife.

SARA: How would *you* know, lump?

PARCH: I been near wives.

CALNE: We'll walk the children back to the house. Whityard,
    Sara, Bethan, come. The morning light
    will cure all curiosities. Are they hungry?

WHITYARD: They ask for nothing, sir.

CALNE: How do you know?
    You know their word for nothing?

SARA: Every word's their word for nothing.

CALNE: Really,
    you understand them, Sara?

SARA: I understand
    Most things, sir.

CALNE: Then maybe you can help me.
    We'll feed them at the house, then they can tell us
    whose they are, and what's their business here.

PARCH: Their business is with me, sir.

CALNE: Thomas Parch
    a man of business? Now I believe you, Whityard,
    they're green as leaves and leapt down from the stars!
    (*Exit CALNE, SARA, BETHAN, WHITYARD, and the
    CHILDREN.*)

PARCH: Well here's a summary justice in starlight.
    Here's your tea-time soldier Master Calne,
    uninterested in the general wrong and right
    of the War Uncivil, takes it on his self
    to rule how a finder can't be a keeper, no more
    than a vicer be a versa. There's the world
    gone off as eggs.

STANER: Good riddances, Tom Parch.
    A bad find in a worse hole and I'm glad
    he took 'em off. What was you fixin' to do?

PARCH: Fixin' still, Ned Staner, fixin' steady.
    I've not said my goodbyes to my pond-creatures,
    and see a golden fringe to the green clouds.

STANER: I don't see that. I smell it, though. Smell that?

PARCH: I don't smell that, I smell the sea. Hush, Ned,
    here's something coming zig and zag towards us.
    Say nothing of the children...
    (*Enter JUXON, muddy.*)
STANER: What *children,* Tom? I never saw no *children!*
    Not two, not one, not none!
JUXON: Beg your pardon?
STANER: I didn't say nothin', not about no *children.*
PARCH: Driven in, that is, Ned, driven in.
JUXON: Starlight to you two seers and sayers of nothin'!
    Who'd think that in the cold of a corn night,
    the sun forgot, I'd find myself bogged in,
    and laping through the squad all high as here?
PARCH: – Now I have no worries, Ned, he's a Norfolk.
    Nothing sticks if you can't tell words from wind.
STANER: 'Bogged in corn,' he goes!
JUXON: See I dropped my catch.
    See? My catch. Whelks but it makes no odd.
    They went all-out rumbustious and rank.
    Tolls, y'see. Tolls at Soham and Swapham,
    great big thunderin' toll at your Very St Edmund,
    and what with loss of time and morgs to pay 'em,
    a knell is tolled for all my whelks.
PARCH: Whelks?
JUXON: See? But don't you scoff 'em now. They're gone.
    My name is Juxon and I hail from Lynn.
    Brought my shells down hereabouts, but look:
    they stink and I got lost. I see this huddle
    and thought I'd come and wonder –
STANER: Ain't no wonder!
JUXON: About my way. How I could make it home.
STANER: Walk rapid anywhere, eh Tom?
PARCH: That's so.
    No food to spare in Woolpit, 'less you got
    money on you.
JUXON: Whelks was all my money.
PARCH: And so, your money's bad and you best be gone.
    that way's London, that way's woodland,

that way's woodland, that way's Stedmunds,
that way's Heaven, and that, we believe round here,
is where your mother had you. Drink to the six
ways to go in the world, Norfolk, and go one.

JUXON: All thirsty men are poor men,
answerin' one sad sip with a sea of thanks.

STANER: On your way, sir, swim your whelks to market!

JUXON: That I might do, sir, that I might do.

(*Exit JUXON, but he stays nearby.*)

STANER: As I was sayin', Tom, 'bout the *white* children...
There, he's gone.

PARCH: Moon's had a glut of strangers.
Now, they've not gone far, and we both know where.
What say we follow, and as we amble there,
I'll work the plan in my brain, you will hear it ticking:
do not be alarmed, young Ned, but continue ambling
as nothing at all was happening.

STANER: Oh I wish
that nothing at all was happening and had already
happened, Tom, and that nothing was yet to happen.
Forward and back and along I would look to nothing
to keep my life as I'd have it. Now you have these
visitors I'm wondering ever where is it,
my peace of mind? It's in pieces, Tom, in the corn.

PARCH: The ticking is beginning, Ned. Walk on.
Tick, tick, tick...

(*Exit PARCH and STANER. Re-enter JUXON.*)

JUXON: They lie so loudly all they tell is truth.
I *did* see what I thought in a green breath.
Holding hands, they was, wept in the corn,
but when I – they was gone.
They *were* the colour I saw.
Man'd need twenty lives to see 'em again.
I'll hurry home to Lynn,
and thank that I saw them once, and I did that.
I'll call them charms for fortune when I fish.
I'll call today a date I never forget.
When it comes I'll wish on it.

Scene Four

Calne's house at Wicks. That night.

(The GREEN GIRL, the GREEN BOY. Enter CALNE, with bread and milk which he sets down near them.)

CALNE: This is for you as children lost at night,
no matter what you seem. Will you not try it?
Whatever you are, it's yours. Will you say nothing,
look, you are in the warm now, in my firelight,
there's no threat here. Will you eat?

GIRL: Somartang, ay?

CALNE: What did you say?

GIRL: Somartang esgan, ay.

CALNE: Is that your name? Mine is Richard Calne.
Richard Calne.

GIRL: Nui, issomartang, ay.

CALNE: Martang – Martin – St Martin?
St Martin, you say?

GIRL: *(To the BOY.)*   Esgany, cheruda, nui.

CALNE: Eat, now, yes? St Martin, yes, St Martin.
(He moves the food to them. The GIRL takes a piece of bread, sniffs it and passes it to the BOY. He tastes it, spits it out, and throws it away.)
Well that was food enough for the five thousand
but clear too much for you. It's milk you need.
(The GIRL tries the milk and spits it out.)
A cat at the touch of water. This is food
nobody doesn't want. Will you not help me?
Whose secret are you? What can you share with us?
(To the BOY.) There's nothing in your eyes that's ever seen
my kind or wanted to, but I see you,
(To the GIRL.) I see you and I think you are – are with us,
you know, you've seen – what, did my mind blow out?
You're foreigners, or offspring of some baron
foul as all the rest –
(Enter BETHAN with broth and SARA with an apple.)
                    Can you believe
no need for bread or milk? What have you brought them?

BETHAN: Broth of the woods, sir, all of the forest herbs,
    them being from somewhere such.
SARA: You feed them that
    they'll speak all right, though probably not to thank you.
CALNE: Sara, what's your gift?
SARA: Only the apple,
    ought to spark some memories, or at least
    some scarlet in their cheeks.
BETHAN: You mean your cheeks
    if it was his you really meant it for.
SARA: You hush.
BETHAN: You hush then.
CALNE: Children, will you try?
    (*The CHILDREN reject both the broth and the apple.*)
SARA: Perhaps you'll have it, sir.
CALNE: (*Taking the apple.*)   Thank you, I shall.
    So. I'm at a loss now. What do you think?
BETHAN: From awful far away, and very lonely.
    The moon, I said, but Sara –
SARA: I said no, sir.
    Badly reared and maybe they lapped poison
    in London wells.
CALNE: The words are not of London.
    This is a music of no place I know.
SARA: Like that of pigs but no one calls that music.
    (*Enter WHITYARD.*)
WHITYARD: Here's honey from my amiables the bees,
    Master Richard. What it lacks in muchness,
    it makes up in a sweetness much exceeding.
CALNE: Thank you, Whityard. What's awake in the village?
WHITYARD: None, it's quiet as like it built itself.
    There's Parch and Staner slurping in the barn
    the Harvest ale amid a dozen sleepers.
    Tom says he's got a plan to feed his children.
CALNE: He has no claim, but if he can he's welcome.
    (*To the GIRL.*) Try this honey, my dear.
    (*The GIRL pushes it away violently.*)
WHITYARD: Too sweet to save you.

SARA: So let them pick and choose their way to death.

If I was green with hunger I'd eat earth.

Ungrateful, isn't she, sir, with all you're doing?

CALNE: It makes no sense.

BETHAN: There's Tom and Ned approaching.

CALNE: Have they brought food?

BETHAN: Tom's armed himself with ale.

SARA: My husband's brought a plentitude of nothing.

BETHAN: They're bad for the children, sir, they'll be no use.

(*Enter PARCH with a tankard of beer, and STANER with nothing.*)

PARCH: Wrong there, Bethan Coley, wrong. I come

flagon-in-hand to help. I was the one

who found these children, I know how to feed 'em.

BETHAN: You brought no food.

PARCH: I brought the food of the gods!

Or the only gods who ever believed in Tom.

CALNE: You'd feed them ale?

PARCH: Well, ale is only water,

Queen of Nature, and the froth by sunlight

Her twinkling coronet, and her robes of green!

CALNE: Try then, try anything.

PARCH: Here, my children.

Swallow a heaven down!

(*The BOY spits it over PARCH.*)

SARA: He spat a hell!

PARCH: God's blood, no child of mine, can't take his ale!

STANER: Ha, Tom Parch, he don't believe your gods!

PARCH: Heathen little toads.

SARA: So how about your offering, Edmond Staner?

STANER: My offering, dear?

CALNE: We're trying to feed these children,

Ned, that's why I asked you here. If you came

with nothing, go with nothing.

STANER: I – got these!

Beans, you see. They're – green. That was my thinkin'

so it ain't, you villagers, nothin', it's, like, somethin'.

(*STANER offers the beans to the CHILDREN. They rip through the stalks and, finding nothing, howl anew.*)

BETHAN: They took to them at first!

SARA: But they prefer
ripping things to eating.

CALNE: Children, see,
it's here, the food is here,
in this, this is the food you eat, the bean...
(*The CHILDREN try, succeed, and begin to eat.*)

CALNE: You saw, they swallowed!

GIRL: Izaghee, masu!

BOY: Ovaka!

GIRL: Saci la! Puluska, puluska!

BOY: Puluska, caloo!

SARA: They want more, Master Richard.
Look... (*To the CHILDREN.*) Puluska?

GIRL: Puluska, ae mani!

SARA: (*Pointing to the beanstalks.*) Puluska, ar?

GIRL: Ae, puluska matoro!

CALNE: Sara, you know a word, the door's ajar!

STANER: Oh yes, that's fair, there's me, I bring the food,
and he's all hugging my wife for how she says
some word that ain't.

CALNE: Run out and fetch in beans!
It's Ned who cracked it! Yes, and you, Tom Parch!

SARA: An hour of him should harvest half a pod.
(*Exit BETHAN and WHITYARD.*)

PARCH: Good work there, Ned.
Two starving freaks? Nothing to any man.
Fat and fit? At home in Tom's New Plan.
And I'm who found 'em.

STANER: Yes, and I'm who fed 'em!

PARCH: We'll rhyme with 'green' and 'bean' from here to autumn!
(*Exit PARCH and STANER.*)

CALNE: Children, more is coming. What was the word?

SARA: Puluska – more, I reckon. Listen... *Food.*
Food.

GIRL: Vood. Puluska?

SARA: Ae, puluska.
More food.

GIRL:　　　　　Mar vood.

CALNE:　　　　　　　　Sara, this goes fast...

SARA: I was pretty sharp in learning, Master Richard.

CALNE: Could you do more? Stay with them, try to learn
　　their – language?

SARA:　　　　　　　Why? We ought to learn them ours.

CALNE: Learn them – teach them ours?

SARA:　　　　　　　　　　Stay in this house?

CALNE: Yes – until – stay here with them?

SARA:　　　　　　　　　　I shall.
　　I'll be the mistress of your little school,
　　won't I, children, won't I?

CALNE:　　　　　　　I believe
　　she understands and knows. She's beautiful.

SARA: I'll teach her words to help her with that, sir.
　　The little angel.

Act Two: Autumn

Scene One

The Wolfpit. Misty autumn night.

SONG

Sloes and cider, pigs and bloodlet,
 Over and ember
 Over and ember
In by the door when the frost is moonlit,
 White is the fruit
 White is the fruit
White is the fruit on the bones of summer.

Plums and damsons, quince and offal,
 Over and ember
 Over and ember
Stagger in cold with the last of the windfall,
 Black is the wind,
 Black is the wind,
Black is the wind through the bones of summer.

Flames and stories, witch and whisper,
 Over and ember
 Over and ember
Eyes of the dead in the cackling timber,
 Gone is her love,
 Gone is her love,
Gone is her love as the bones of summer.

Friends and frenzies, ale and firelight,
 Over and ember
 Over and ember
Dance to my arms in the mist at midnight,
 Bright is our fire,
 Bright is our fire,
Bright is our fire with the bones of summer!

(*PARCH is staggering home. Parson DEAZIL has just got up.*)

PARCH: Dance is over, parson, like the summer,
and all of your parishioners hereabouts
are face down on the floor of the wheat-barn
and crunching on the lattermath. You're late.

DEAZIL: I am not late for anything, Tom Parch,
I'm early for all things. I've left my bed
to start the day.

PARCH: We had it,
you missed it. Now you will dwell in a yesterday
all your life, and I'll be the veriest prophet,
twittering from my nest in a blue tomorrow.

DEAZIL: See that star, Tom Parch? It's the morning-star.

PARCH: Parson, see that hedge? It's the midnight-hedge,
and I should know. I spent
an hour in consultation with its brambles.

DEAZIL: Perhaps I'll stand with you until the sun
mocks this idle fancy.

PARCH: He won't mock it.
He and I go backward, parson. No,
and you'll not stand so long with a safe soul.

DEAZIL: What makes you think your soul is safe?

PARCH: I saved it.
I saved it for a better class of parson.

DEAZIL: Fruitless nonsense from a cider barrel.

PARCH: A drunken one, then, if it's lost its fruit.

DEAZIL: I'll wait until the sky can prove me right.

PARCH: Spoken like a true Christian churchman.
You'd better get to bed before some crow
starts quoting you.

DEAZIL: I've just got out of bed!

PARCH: You having trouble sleeping? Me too.
Can't close my eyes without I see green things.

DEAZIL: What's that – green things?

PARCH: That's nought but a bad dream.

DEAZIL: No not a dream, but something I've been hearing
these several weeks.

PARCH: Good evening to you, parson.

DEAZIL: Good morning but stay there, Tom Parch! Is it true
That soldier up at Wicks is harbouring two

Freaks of creatures found on the last day
Of Harvest?

PARCH: That's a tale
a Dutchman couldn't spout with a straight face.
Too many late nights, parson.

DEAZIL: I believe
I've trod the serpent's tail: it's the Devil's vanguard!

PARCH: A dream it was, that you call Devil, parson.
No green child could be as green as your
envisagings.

DEAZIL: Ah-ha! You said a child!

PARCH: I said so in the night.

DEAZIL: But in the day
I overhear it!

PARCH: Parson,
some morning we'll rise up in a day together,
get to know each other, like, but until –
good night to all your days.

DEAZIL: Good day to all
your swollen nights, Tom Parch. – You've drunk so much
your secret's spilt at the brim. Now for the soldier.

Scene Two

Calne's house at Wicks. That day.

(*SARA, the GREEN GIRL, slightly faded, the GREEN BOY not.*)

SARA: Again, Say it again.

GIRL: I set in master reechas ghows esarra.

SARA: 'With Sara.'

GIRL: Wit sara.

SARA: 'With Sara of the beautiful long hair,' try…

GIRL: Wit sara of te –

SARA: Never mind. Say this: 'Here is my brother.'

GIRL: Heeres mabrana.

SARA: Whatever the hell he is. He never says.
He never says a word but 'stone'. Do you?
Oi, do you?

BOY: Zton, ezton.

SARA: Stone, that's right, you stick with that. Now you:
   'My hands, my head, my heart.'

GIRL: Muyanz, muyaid, muyark.

SARA: My 'heart', feel...

GIRL: Muy hart, ae.

SARA: Ba-boom, ba-boom.

GIRL: Ba-boom, ba-boom. Muyart. Cheruda, muyart!

BOY: Zton, es sang ezton.

SARA: Nothing to do with stone, you moss of a child.
   Now see, here's what you drew. Draw it again.
   Draw me your – St Martinsland, your home...
   Hills, fine, and some animals in a field.
   Cows, are they? Sky. Clouds. The trees.
   Then, far away, that line. That line again.
   What is this line? What's below the line?

GIRL: Ymar. Ymar saci. Esgany sarra.

SARA: The sea, you live by the sea – what colour's the sea?

GIRL: Is greenas. Clows is greenas.

SARA: The sun? The sun? Give me the chalk, I'll do it,
   crowned and shining, there! Sun! What is this?
   ...Nothing doing. Blank as the thing itself.
   Too bad, but nowhere doesn't have a sun.
   Fine, I suppose that nowhere is your home.

GIRL: Home. Home es war es sang estone.

SARA: 'Song of stone' again there. Song of stone...
   (*Enter CALNE.*)

SARA: Here's the master. What do you say to the master?

GIRL: Good morning to ye lord.

CALNE: Well, good morning!

GIRL: Ur wass to go war sea is, lord.

SARA: She learnt
   'sea' and 'sky'. I think she lives by a shore,
   she drew that place. I drew the sun myself,
   she wouldn't have it. 'Song of stone,' she goes.
   And nothing from the boy
   but 'stone' itself.

GIRL: Sang estone by ulfpit.

SARA: Woolpit. No one saw a wolf in our time.

CALNE: How can I thank you?

SARA: Oh, I love my work.
I could teach the willow to speak oak.
But sir, you have to see… Look at them together.
They're not the same, I'm sure of it. He's greener,
or else she's lightened half a shade, like she's
in sunshine, he's in shadow.

CALNE: She's the one
who's eaten bread and apples. This poor clod
dwells in his den of beans and water.

SARA: And stone.
He barely talks to her now, let alone
his teacher. What does it mean?
I'm helping you, aren't I?

CALNE: More than I thought –
(*A knock at the door.*)
The woman's in the forest. Run and see.
(*Exit SARA.*)
The sea then, is it? Well, that's far away.
Your new home is a long walk from the sea.

GIRL: Home. How is home?

CALNE: Home is here.
My home, yours, the village of Woolpit. Here.
Home is with me, Adela. Say it, Adela…

GIRL: Adela.

CALNE: Home is with Richard.

GIRL: Sang estone.

BOY: Ezton, ezton –

CALNE: Be quiet!
(*Enter SARA.*)

SARA: Beggar at your gate. A rosy rich one.

CALNE: Rich beggar, what do you mean?

SARA: I mean a church one,
begging to have your time. The parson, Deazil,
our holy man of Bury.

CALNE: Hide the children,
Quick, he's been already, he thinks –
(*Enter DEAZIL.*)

114

DEAZIL: I think
your serving girl has failed to bar the door,
but thus she shows respect for a holy man.
(*CALNE signals for SARA to go.*)
CALNE: This is the work of a holy man these days?
To step in uninvited?
DEAZIL: – Oh my word…
What leaked into this house?
CALNE: They have no names.
DEAZIL: I know some names. What are they?
CALNE: Gypsy children.
DEAZIL: Where did you find them, sir?
CALNE: They were near the wolfpit.
Some reapers found them in the last of Harvest.
DEAZIL: Extraordinary, this – malady. Can one touch them?
CALNE: Yes, so it's not a malady, is it, parson?
DEAZIL: The Abbey won't accept that. It's a sickness.
CALNE: Why tell the Abbey? They're children, they're lost children.
DEAZIL: That's what you say they are. What do *they* say?
Do they say anything English?
CALNE: Nothing English,
nothing we understand. I say they are gypsies.
Healthy, though. Of that I'm sure.
DEAZIL: You're sure?
Colour aside, are they normal, though, in – form?
CALNE: I think so.
DEAZIL: You don't know? You never looked?
CALNE: I did. They are. I saw them in their sleep.
DEAZIL: Oh? And what do they eat?
CALNE: What do they eat?
The boy eats only beans the colour he is,
but she eats half the stuff we set for her.
DEAZIL: Half the stuff, half gypsy, half a child …
Look at her. If it wasn't for the sickness
she might be quite the flower of Suffolk. But.
She isn't, is she? More's the pity, no?
CALNE: Nobody has to see or know these children.
DEAZIL: On the contrary, I do. You were charged, sir,

to appraise me of all things unnatural.
You've signally failed in that.
CALNE: They're not unnatural.
DEAZIL: They're off to market, are they?
CALNE: Isn't it clear
they're nothing from the war? What, are they barons?
DEAZIL: Who knows? We are hearing nightmares in the day,
of riders without names, of houses burning
without fire, they say as close as Essex.
You're right to have no part in it all, I'm sure.
CALNE: It's why I keep these children here with me.
DEAZIL: You keep them here with you. I'm glad you do,
it's kind of you, but nothing is that simple.
I was in Bury yesterday –
CALNE: You told them?
DEAZIL: Only the Sacrist –
CALNE: Why then waste my time?
Build a pyre, why not?
DEAZIL: No, you mistake me.
The Sacrist sent me here to oversee
immediate baptism of these foundlings
under cover of night. Do you understand me?
He thinks it best to avoid at the present time
a spectacle, but we need the ritual done.
CALNE: I have to keep them here for their protection.
Some would have them cast out or beaten.
DEAZIL: A thoroughly rosy view of the world you have.
Some would have 'em burned alive
if they could see what I see. Half the cloister,
I'm not a guessing man.
CALNE: I can refuse.
DEAZIL: Oh my. Ho-dee. You can't.
CALNE: They're in my home.
DEAZIL: And where, sir, is your home?
The Liberty of the Abbey of St Edmund.
The Abbey owns the land, the sky, the air,
the folk who breathe it. Thus it owns the breath
you're taking now, and now it owns your sigh.

What's yours preceded birth and will follow death:
God's, in other words. While we abide here,
joyous in the Liberty of St Edmund,
we are mere handled treasures of the saint.
Understand?

CALNE: You say under cover of night.

DEAZIL: On Sunday, yes.

CALNE: And what will you tell your Sacrist?

DEAZIL: Oh, I couldn't better *your* tale, sir, all
swollen hearts and trickling eyes! 'There was once
a soldier who took pity of two gypsies,
and no one knew but him and the simple farmers,
and, of course, your humble servant...' Sunday night,
a baptism, and then,
we do not want to see these two again.
Not unless they look the way we're, well,
accustomed to, Master Calne. Do you understand that?
You ought to thank me. Well. I bid you adieu.
(*Exit DEAZIL.*)

CALNE: Don't be afraid, it's nothing.
Words in a church. Where St Martin is.

GIRL: Sommartin?

CALNE: That's right, your friend. Don't worry. I'll protect you.
I won't be long, Adela, and when I do this
it means I'll be back soon.
(*CALNE kisses her as he leaves.*)

BOY: Emaru, zaia, emaru!

GIRL: Tha sol greenas.
Is greenas. Now I zay, 'Hallo Sarra,
good mornet.' And I zay, 'Here is my land.
Here is my land I komen fram to ulfpit.
Now ulfpit is my land is not of greenas.'

BOY: Ezton, ezton. Sang ezton. Saci-la.

GIRL: 'Is wass who knows? Now engish is my land.'

BOY: Nui, nui, nui!

GIRL: Is engish alwess!

BOY: Nui!
(*The BOY is very agitated. Enter SARA. He goes quiet.*)

SARA: Adela, my. The flower of the season.
GIRL: Sarra, hallo, good mornet. This is my land.
    (*She shows SARA the chalk drawing.*)
SARA: It's full of people now. But it's not green,
    they look like us –
GIRL: There's Sarra, there's Richatt –
SARA: Who's that with Richard, smiling, it's not Sara –
GIRL: Is very bright, is nothing ever greenas –
SARA: The sun's come out –
GIRL: We alwess have the sonn –
SARA: It's not your land, it's mine, you stupid thing –
GIRL: Is engand we af kom away to ulfpit –
    (*SARA rubs out the drawing and grabs the GIRL's hand.*)
SARA: It's England? Give me your hand – You call this England?
    These English eyes, these Suffolk ears, this mouth
    a Woolpit gob? Your name is not Adela.
    You're something of a trick. I think you're laughing…
    You know more than you're saying, I reckon, and I know
    more than what you think. We haven't finished
    our lesson yet. You need more than a picture
    and half a dozen words to stand with Richard
    in sunlight, don't you know? I'm going to show you
    how we get baptised in Sara's manner,
    with songs and dances of the month of blood.
    You'll be like me, a Christian in November.
    I'm going to bring an angel to the altar,
    my darling. Now, follow, after teacher…

Scene Three

Woolpit, Martinmas. By the woods. Night.

(*PARCH, STANER. They are splashed with blood.*)

STANER: Blood enough for puddings all the way
    to Christmas Eve.
PARCH: Let's see… Not so, Ned Staner,
    not with the hungers of a hearty man.
    With luck December first.

STANER: But here's some months
   of Martinmas red meat, eh, Tom?

PARCH: Some months?
   I'd say a week.

STANER: You better watch it, Tom.
   Next year they'll drive you in the wood yourself
   and feed you on beechmast and acorns! See,
   mistaking you for a pig, I mean.

PARCH: I know
   the gist of what you mean. That Tom-is-a-pig-
   so-feed-him-acorns joke has been a regular
   feature of St Martinmas since first
   I was by God allotted a hayrake
   for company.

STANER: You always say hayrake,
   Tom, you always get your own back.

PARCH: Well,
   if I think of something scrawnier next year
   I'll change my tune.

STANER: You'll never change your tune.
   You're stuck with it!

PARCH: And here comes what you're stuck with.
   (*Enter SARA.*)

SARA: Who slaughtered who, or did the swine survive?

STANER: Here I am, my dear, providing all
   our winter needs.

SARA: I ache for needless summer.

PARCH: What's new at the soldier's manor, Mistress Staner?
   He turning green yet, or he turning soldier?

SARA: He walks about and stops and stares at her.
   Him he hardly bothers with. Me neither.
   Stone is all his language, and he never
   moves except to palm a string of beans
   into his gob. But her –
   she's learning what I'm teaching.

STANER: What you teachin'?

SARA: Oh, woman things, you know.

STANER: Ah, woman things.

SARA: I'd say she's yellowing to ladyhood.

STANER: Yellow is she? I seen yellow persons.

PARCH: So what's his plan with them? If all he does
    is fence and feed 'em, I say give 'em back
    to him who found 'em – *me* – and him who found out
    how to feed 'em – *him* – so we can start
    like putting them to work.

SARA: To work, Tom Parch?

PARCH: Nothing, mistress. Man things, man things.

SARA: Won't get no work from them, they're idiots.
    He's dead to life, and her she just repeats.
    Richard makes a tale of it.

STANER: 'Richard'?
    He calls you 'Sara', does he?

SARA: It is my name.

STANER: It is her name, she goes.

PARCH: It *is* her name.

STANER: Well, *I* know what I mean.

PARCH: I'm glad you do,
    else all your meaning sobs a mile from home.

SARA: I'll leave you butcher-clowns to your blood time.
    I had some news for you of a green baptism,
    but so, I'll go alone.

PARCH: A green baptism?

SARA: They're children, no?

PARCH: Baptism when?

SARA: Tonight,
    in secret at St Mary's. Deazil came,
    the Abbey wants them christened, and then hidden,
    hidden away.

PARCH: They'll not be hid from me.
    I'm with you, Mistress Sara, I'm for church.

SARA: I better show you where it is, Tom Parch.

STANER: Tom, we had enough of them green troubles.

PARCH: Ned, the plan... Nothing's too much troubles
    if it's part two or three or nine in a plan.

SARA: Come on, you brave crusaders, all your pigs
    are Christians now, and all your puddings holy.

Scene Four

St Mary Woolpit. That night. Moonlight through stained glass.

(*Procession: DEAZIL, CALNE, the CHILDREN, BETHAN, SARA and WHITYARD. PARCH and STANER hide themselves.*)

STANER: Even in God's house, look Tom they're green!

PARCH: You're more or less as yellow as you were outside the door.

STANER: They're red, they're violet colour – demons!

PARCH: Moonlight through the glass, you dullard.

DEAZIL: Whom do you call the Godparents, sir?

CALNE: Myself and Bethan Coley.

DEAZIL: Then step forward.
Dearly beloved, forasmuch as all men are conceived and born in sin, and that our Saviour Christ saith, none can enter into the Kingdom of God, except he be regenerate and born anew of Water and the Holy Ghost: I beseech you to call upon God the Father, through our Lord Jesus Christ, that of his bounteous mercy he will grant to these children that thing which by nature they cannot have –
(*The GIRL is transfixed by the light of the stained glass on her skin.*)

GIRL: Greenas, raadas, greenas, raadas.
I kom down from se enjels.

DEAZIL: Restrain them.

CALNE: Hush, Adela.

DEAZIL: Let us pray…

GIRL: I kom from by se enjels.

DEAZIL: What did she say?

CALNE: Her language, nothing, parson.

DEAZIL: Almighty and everlasting God, who of thy great mercy didst save Noah and his family in the ark from perishing by water…

GIRL: I lof you are as enjels.

CALNE: Be quiet.

DEAZIL: I thought she had no English.

CALNE: It's not English.

I did the thing you asked, I kept my word.

Will you not baptise the children?

DEAZIL: Also, didst safely lead the Children of Israel thy people through the Red Sea...

GIRL: The sea, the sea is brad is an nu sonn,

the day is alwess ended.

DEAZIL: What does she mean?

Do they originate in darkness?

CALNE: Adela,

be quiet. How do I know?

(*The BOY begins to sing an unearthly song, and the GIRL gently to sway.*)

DEAZIL: Almighty and immortal God, the aid of all that need, the helper of all that flee to thee for succour, the life of them that believe, and the resurrection of the dead: We call upon thee for these children – stop him, sir!

CALNE: Parson, he's a child. You drown his singing with words of God. Is that not what you're here for?

DEAZIL: That they, coming to Holy Baptism, may receive remission for their sins by spiritual regeneration. Ask, and ye shall have – (he can't do that!) – seek, and ye shall find – (not in this church!) – knock, and it shall be opened to you: So now give unto us that ask – (I demand you stop his screeching, sir!) – let us that seek find; open the gate unto us that knock...that – knock – I command you, sir, to stop his infernal howling!

CALNE: Baptise them, man!

DEAZIL: He fouls the air with song!

CALNE: Parson, I kept my word, now you keep yours!

DEAZIL: Bring her.

(*CALNE brings the GIRL to DEAZIL. The BOY continues to sing.*)

Wilt thou be baptised in this faith?

CALNE: That is my desire.

DEAZIL: Name this child.

CALNE: Adela.

DEAZIL: I baptise thee in the Name of the Father, and of the Son, and of the Holy Ghost, amen. We receive this child into the Congregation of Christ's flock, and do sign her with the sign of the Cross. Give me the boy.

(*As CALNE does so, and DEAZIL lets the GIRL loose, she begins to dance among them. CALNE, BETHAN, SARA and WHITYARD start to lose control of themselves. The BOY sings on as they try to baptise him.*)

DEAZIL: Name this child.

CALNE: John.

DEAZIL: What?

CALNE: John!

DEAZIL: I baptise thee in the Name of the Father, and of the Son, and of the Holy Ghost, amen. We receive this child into the Congregation of Christ's flock, and do sign her with the sign of the Cross, in token that hereafter he shall not be ashamed to confess the faith of Christ crucified, and manfully to fight under his banner against sin, the world, and the devil –

GIRL: Green defil am I, green enjel am I, master!

DEAZIL: – Christ's faithful soldier and servant unto his life's end, amen...

GIRL: Master I am green enjel I am green defil!
I lof you and I lof you and I lof you!
(*She leaps upon DEAZIL and dances wildly among them. PARCH and STANER emerge from hiding, enchanted.*)

DEAZIL: They're heathens, I won't have it!

CALNE: She doesn't know, she doesn't know what she's saying!

DEAZIL: *In nomine Patris, et Filii, et Spiritus Sancti, amen – per virtutem Domini sint medicina mei pia Crux Virgo Maria mihi succurre, et defende ab omni maligno spiritu... Ah – gi – la – cah –*

CALNE: That's not a prayer, it's a curse!

DEAZIL: It's a spell against!
Tetragrammaton, Alpha! Oh she's an angel!

CALNE: Adela, stop –

GIRL: I lof you, I am an enjel!

WHITYARD: She says she loves me!

STANER: It's me, oh Tom, I'm burning!
    She's calling to me!

PARCH: It's me, it's Tom she's saying!

DEAZIL: *Ooo, Primogenitus! Vita, vita, sapiencia!*
    (*They are in wild confusion, which ends when the BOY's song
    ends, and the GIRL stops dancing. The VILLAGERS look
    about in bewilderment.*)

CALNE: What, is this abbey turned
    abattoir with farmers? What are you doing
    sweating here?

PARCH: I'd as soon ask you why
    you dance the way you do, sir.

CALNE: Why I – what?

WHITYARD: Now it's a dream for sure, I can say as I please,
    and no one blame me tomorrow! What that makes me
    is King of the Dreamers!

DEAZIL: I – I – Master Calne,
    these are unearthly matters I must bring
    immediately to the monks –

PARCH: That's a grand idea,
    parson, but be sure to tell 'em *you* danced
    the way you did with her, or else *I* shall,
    so unforget'ble a sight it were.

DEAZIL: I'm sure
    the monks will credit a drunken wretch.

CALNE: No, parson,
    they might believe me, though. But I'll say nothing
    if you say nothing. You came here to baptise them.
    They are baptised, are they not?

DEAZIL: I warn you, Master Soldier, lock them away.
    Erase them from the records of this town.
    And I'll forget I ever saw them, I ever –
    I ever saw her – saw her –
    (*Exit DEAZIL, confused.*)

CALNE: You'd all be wise to do as the parson does.
    Forget you saw them, forget
    they ever came here. They belong to me now,
    Understand? Come John, Adela. Home.

(*Exit CALNE, the GIRL and the BOY.*)

WHITYARD: Well if I dream, I sleep, so I'm not tired.
    I'll haunt my kingdom in the dark.

BETHAN: Good night,
    Sara. What did you teach her?

SARA: Me, oh nothing.
    Nothing that's done me any good.

BETHAN: Then I'm sorry.
    I hope it's done her some, but it's only hope.
    (*Exit WHITYARD and BETHAN.*)

PARCH: We have to have them pixies off the soldier.

STANER: But Tom, she does these things!

PARCH: She does indeed,
    and, tell the truth, she does 'em to me too.
    Who wouldn't pay to know her better, Ned?

STANER: I want to know her better!

PARCH: That you shall.
    You ask your wife permission.

STANER: Tom I forgot her!

PARCH: I'll leave you, Ned, to your thoughts.
    – Hey, Mistress Staner, reckon that's the end
    of all your schooling.

SARA: Looks like it.

PARCH: No more
    rainy afternoons at the manor.

SARA: He wants her,
    it's clear as day, he wants his toe in the pond.

PARCH: Now what he wants is a hide of a certain shade,
    eh Sara, see what I'm saying? That could be you,
    the hide of a certain shade. You walk with me,
    I think we pinkish folk could make each other's
    dream come true this winter. You walk with Tom.

Act Three: Winter

Scene One

Calne's house at Wicks. The night of New Year's Eve.

(*BETHAN and the GREEN CHILDREN. The GIRL, again, has faded in colour.*)

SONG

BETHAN: *The apple's eaten, the year is died,*
The sun is climbing over the side,
   The robin's flown the ocean wide,
    Remember me, forget me.

   Gather in rings and part in pairs,
   And ring the days and part the years,
    Twinkle in another's tears,
     Remember me, forget me.

   Old Year left my love for dead,
   New Year see me wooed and wed,
    For all that's said will soon be said

BETHAN
/ GIRL: *Remember me, forget me.*

BETHAN: *Fresh is dawn and pale and rose*
   With blood of Time, but no one knows
    Where Time or Love or Laughter goes,

BETHAN
/ GIRL: *Remember me, forget me.*

BETHAN: *The apple's eaten, the year is died,*
The sun is climbing over the side,
   The robin's flown the ocean wide,

BETHAN
/ GIRL: *Remember me, forget me.*

BETHAN: See how it's gone, Adela, but it's not gone.
GIRL: The year is died.

BETHAN: Yes, but it soon begins,
 it dies and begins again at the stroke of midnight.
 Twelve chimes you'll hear close by at Mary Woolpit,
 then far away at Bury, where the monks
 are ages old and wise.

GIRL: The year is died
 and born them many time.

BETHAN: Many times, Adela.

GIRL: Poor old years.

BETHAN: Poor years.

GIRL: And where they gone?

BETHAN: They find a place, the years.

GIRL: There is no sun.
 The sea is green. Is far away all bright.

BETHAN: Where's that, Adela?

GIRL: Poor year, he live by a light,
 is only light as is it not a darkness.
 An war he is all light is ever so,
 as in an East wan night is at his end,
 as in a West wan day is. But is brightness
 over a braad old river. There is a land
 is sky is always brightly shining over.
 Poor old year is say is land of Jesus.

BETHAN: Is that – your home, Adela?

GIRL: Here is home.
 I kom to Martinsland and I were poisont.
 Turn me to green.

BETHAN: Green? No, nearly golden!

GIRL: (*At BOY.*) He poisont and he dum. He all is stone
 he green as snakes.

BETHAN: He's ill, dear.

GIRL: Poor old year.
 Remember him forget him
 (*A knock at the door. BETHAN rises.*)

GIRL: Middlenight.

BETHAN: Not yet. Some beggar, maybe.
 (*Enter SARA.*)

BETHAN: Sara, you're not at the dancing?

SARA: Sure
    I'm at the dancing, here's a dance that threw me
    out of the barn, oh me I'm always dancing
    if anyone would see it. But you, Bethan,
    you should be at the dancing.
BETHAN: It's the children,
    with Master Calne gone up to Swadringham
    to see his brother, I'm staying with the children.
SARA: Top of the evening, tail of the year to you two,
    Yellowfinch and Stonechat. Look it's Sara,
    remember me? I used to be your teacher,
    but now I'm all unwelcome, I'm a whiteskin,
    I'm not allowed near angels.
BETHAN: Oh you are, though,
    surely? Here, it's Sara.
SARA: It's not Sara,
    it's Mrs Staner, my full name being
    Happy-New-Year-to-You-*Mrs*-Staner, the meaning:
    they'll dance with no one married. They're all saying,
    'Where's young Bethan Coley, the village beauty?'
BETHAN: You're saying that.
SARA: 'She's free, she's sweet and comely,
    ain't she, Bethan Coley?'
BETHAN: Sweet, they're saying?
    What do they know?
SARA: Nothing, while you sit here
    combing the gloomy goddess, nothing at all.
    I'll sit with these, I'm done with Dead Year Ending.
    There's no new year for Sara, just an old one
    and a haggard husband snoring in it.
BETHAN: The master,
    Sara, it's him who said –
SARA: Oh he'll be hours,
    him drinking with his brother. You go along
    and spin the befuddled heads – 'seemly,' they said,
    and 'innocent,' they mentioned.
BETHAN: Innocent?
    They ought to get to know me!

SARA: So they ought.
 I'll sit with my old friends.
BETHAN: I'm awful thankful,
 Sara.
SARA: So am I, missing them bad,
 I was, I was. Go, rake the pile for husbands.
 (*Exit BETHAN.*)
SARA: You *do* remember, don't you, I'm the bringer
 of nothing but good news. You have a date,
 you, Yellowfinch, tonight, with a white master
 you'll drop upon from Heaven.
GIRL: Poor old year
 is died.
SARA: Not yet, he hasn't, you and I
 we'll go and hunt him, shall we, with a quiver?
GIRL: Poor old year forget me.
SARA: You forget him,
 we'll roast you up the skin of a new lovebird
 and then you'll eat all night a meat with sauces.
 Meantime, say howdee to a green half-uncle.
 (*SARA opens the window for PARCH, who is smeared with
 green.*)
PARCH: Halloo, hallay, good dye to yow, kinswoman!
 Yow kom with me and have a foin old time,
 for I be old St Martin, Martin Willow!
SARA: A joke too late, she's in the shire of yellow.
PARCH: But I'm also known as the Bishop of Buttercup,
 account of my changing hue. Sometimes –
SARA: Shut up
 and let's get out. He won't be gone forever.
 Where's Ned?
PARCH: At work on the Green Plan, Mistress Staner,
 the same as me, if you look, so don't you worry.
 We'll have his angel home before next year.
GIRL: Iss Sara. Poor oh angels. Poor oh angels.
 I love you of all angels.
PARCH: Well that is handy,
 'cause they love all of yow, and specially him
 who'll love yow for a price.

SARA: Let's go, Adela,
    We're going to stalk the angels.
    (*SARA starts to lead the GIRL away. The BOY follows.*)
PARCH: No, not so,
    not you, my friend. We got no room for you,
    we'll get no deal on you.
GIRL: He is all stone,
    an green as snakes is.
SARA: Stay behind, you get it?
    Stay, stay.
    (*The BOY halts, uncertain. Then retreats.*)
PARCH: A message, Mistress Staner,
    you know what scrawl she does.
SARA: It's done already.
    'Dear mastor, is by the pit I am – '
GIRL: Dear master...
SARA: 'Is by the pit I am an wate for Richet.'
    (*PARCH looks at the message.*)
PARCH: You'd best be spelling it wrong.
SARA: It is wrong.
PARCH: Oh.
    – That's excellent in the plan, the spelling it wrong.
SARA: I'll leave this on the door.
PARCH: We'll meet with Ned
    up at the pit, he should have brung the reeve.
SARA: Come on, Adela, nothing like a green girl,
    or not on New Year's Evening.
    (*Exit PARCH, SARA and the GIRL. After a while, the BOY
    follows.*)

Scene Two

The Wolfpit.

(*STANER and WHITYARD.*)

STANER: Here's the place in the plan, the spot to be at.
WHITYARD: I know the spot from an earlier dream. Whenever
    I'm here I say, 'So it wasn't a dream after all!'

Then it ends in dream again. But still, meanwhile,
I'm free as ever I was.
STANER: Do you never think
   the dream's been long, Master reeve, it's been long lasting?
WHITYARD: Contrarily I think it has been both endless
   and barely at all begun.
STANER: I tell you what's next
   is the favourite stretch of the dream.
WHITYARD: It's a dream you know?
STANER: When you were last awake you told me so.
   You said I dreamed I met with Ned the Friend,
   and he was good to me and so was Tom,
   they found me love, and it was deep enduring,
   so I promised them 'one year without no labour'.
WHITYARD: Is that what I promise them?
STANER: You do in the dream.
   No sowing, reaping, slaughtering, scything, nothing.
   You promise it in the dream, out of your gladness.
WHITYARD: And this is about to happen?
STANER: About to happen
   and happen, Master reeve and then re-happen.
WHITYARD: And is it song that brings it forward?
STANER: Song?
   I heard no song.
WHITYARD: Song of the green boy singing.
   Can you not hear that?
STANER: Oh yes, it's in the dreaming.
WHITYARD: And next in time was dancing.
STANER: Oh there's dancing,
   now Tom's at hand with a trophy!
   (*Enter PARCH with the GIRL, who gazes into the pit.*)
STANER: Tom, you're the boss, you got her!
PARCH: Hush your noise,
   and if you call me, call me Martin Willow.
WHITYARD: It happens as you say – I dreamed of her
   from in the dream.
PARCH: Where's he in his Bible, Ned?
STANER: He's Jonah with his dreams. Where's my lady?

PARCH: Stone in her shoe.
STANER: She waiting for us somewhere?
PARCH: She's waiting for her man, Ned, don't trouble.
STANER: Her man, that's me!
PARCH: That's right. Now, Master Whityard,
    you ready for love in the last
    gasp of the groaning year?
WHITYARD: I'm greenly ready.
PARCH: And that's how ready to be. And my assistant he's
    apprised you of our terms for the achieving
    of all this love?
WHITYARD: I dreamed her from the singing.
STANER: 'No sowing, reaping, slaughtering, scything, nothing'
    was how I put it.
PARCH: You missed out carting, cutting,
    nutting, cropping, picking, sorting, sweating,
    all gathering in of herbs and heifers, and all
    being where Tom would sooner *not* be and all
    duties appertaining – what's that silence?
STANER: It's quiet silence, Tom.
PARCH: It's the frog he's at it,
    his hungry note…
WHITYARD: I understand all terms,
    good Master Parch.
PARCH: …I thought I heard the singing…
    It's only me. – We pay you in green coinage,
    you pay us in blue leisure time.
STANER: For a year.
PARCH: No carting and stacking, mind you.
WHITYARD: Here's my hand.
PARCH: And here's its cousin. Say it: 'a year of freedom'.
WHITYARD: A year of freedom, Masters Parch and Staner.
PARCH: I won't say thank you, we've a private yellow
    mouth it does it for us. Off we go now,
    down to the meadow stream we chosen special,
    we laid a cloth along the bank to warm you,
    reeve, and so you spread across a rainbow,
    green to yellow to red!

(*Exit WHITYARD with STANER. STANER comes back
suddenly.*)

STANER: And Tom, you said, Tom,
me after, isn't it, seeing as how I want her?

PARCH: When was it ever anything but you after,
Ned? Now you go after him before he
drowns himself in a dream and says, 'I thought so.'

STANER: I'm going, Tom, I'm gone!

PARCH: And you, my beowty,
you wish your wish and go with Martin Willow!

GIRL: Where Sara?

PARCH: Sara who? Unless you're meaning
she who fled away to the old country,
your state of make-believe. She's in the land
of lay-me-down and lie-to-me. You wouldn't
know her.

GIRL: She forget me.

PARCH: She forget you.
Forget her too, you can.
You're turning white, now turn a good white man!
(*Exit PARCH and the GIRL. Enter SARA, painting her face,
and the BOY who goes to the wolfpit and stares in.*)

SARA: I told you, go away! Who ever heard
I smear this muck on my cheek it makes my shadow
green as it? Go off, you burr, go home!
Ah-hah, it's home he's gone. Recognise it?
Here's where you began to turn this village
to fairyland. I bet you're proud, you must be.
We used to get things done, we were no trouble.
(*He turns and stares at her painting herself. He makes her
uneasy.*)
You like to see a girl turn animal,
do you? Fine, you watch. Who knows, perhaps
you'll tell me how you did it, you and the little
grasshopper, what stuff you used, you little
lying little caterpillars! – Oh,
I'm sure it's not your doing. You're so simple
you don't how to get it off, she's left you

stuck like that, you little moss-ball, you…
You can talk to me in English if you like,
you really can, because even if I told him,
Richard, Richard, he'd not believe me, a rose,
you see, I am, I have no flavour for him,
do I? Go on, talk to me in English,
you pond-pebble, do it. You never liked me
how I was – but don't you love me now?
(*She turns, wholly green. She pulls up her hood. The BOY runs
to her.*)
BOY: Alawi, alawi, cheruda, zharay!
SARA: Get off me,
afflicted thing! Be off, go home!
BOY: Alawi?
SARA: No, whatever, no.
BOY: Amasu?
SARA: Get lost!
(*SARA runs at the BOY who, terrified, jumps back into the pit.*)
Goodbye now, is it? No? Well you stay there
till this old year comes round again, and wolves
are nuzzling at your feet. – A light, he's coming!
What's my name? Adela.
Where'd I come from? Never-ask-me land.
Where am I going? You wouldn't understand it.
What's my name? Adela. I'm your friend.
(*Enter CALNE. He approaches SARA.*)
CALNE: The last night of the year and you came here,
Adela, you came here. Of course you did,
and had I any decency I'd of course
Have brought you here myself. I'm sorry, Adela.
It's cold, you come with me, I think, don't you,
we leave together –
(*SARA grabs CALNE and pulls him down upon her. At first
he resists.*)
Not possible, not right,
I meant to say myself, I meant to say
you're mine, I feel, I – Beautiful Adela,
so far from home, I –

(*SARA silences him again.*)

Tell me, tell me something –

who are you, won't you say? If I'm to know you –

(*The BOY emerges and screams, then sinks back into the pit. They scramble up. SARA runs away.*)

In the name of Christ be quiet! Adela, don't go!

Adela, stay with me, Adela!

(*CALNE goes to the pit's edge.*)

You gurgle through your hole,

you miscreated elf. Adela, come back!

(*CALNE runs off. Enter PARCH, STANER and WHITYARD, drinking.*)

PARCH / STANER / WHITYARD: (*Sing.*)

> *The year's a hag, the night is young,*
> *The thief is stole, the sheep is hung,*
> > *The song is plucked, the carcass sung,*
> > *Remember me forget me!*

> *The year's a man, the night's a maid.*
> *The thief is cooked, the sheep is paid,*
> > *The lady's done, the deed is laid,*
> > *Remember me forget me!*

PARCH: Bring me the fields of heavenly wheat, and a scythe

I'll string a hair across and pluck a tune of,

I got no work to do, not now, not ever!

Now I'm the duke of rest and the lord of slumber!

STANER: A year, it is, Tom Parch.

PARCH: And that's forever.

He's still be in his dream, he'll not remember.

WHITYARD: I like this stretch, I liked the yellow chapter,

the river-girl, but that was over quickly –

PARCH: Speak for yourself, eh reeve!

WHITYARD: I like this amiable

cheeriness that follows.

STANER: Who's being cheery?

I never got my green reward, I trembled

what with the chill and off she was gone.

PARCH: Be thankful,

135

Ned Beanstalk, for she'd not have noticed you
whatever stand you made.

STANER: You got *your* time,
he got *his* time and takes it all for dreaming,
it's only Ned who's stood on the earth with nothing
holding him like that.

PARCH: What's next in Woolpit,
green husbandman Sir Whityard?

WHITYARD: That's the lambing,
Tom, we've the lambing next.

PARCH: In a crow's crevice,
reeve, it's nothing at all, twelve months of nothing!

(*Sings.*) *The year's a babe, the night's a crone,*
The thieves in flocks, the sheep alone,
The crop is shat, the crap is sown,
Remember me forget me!

WHITYARD: There's drums to that.

STANER: Who's running?

(*Enter BETHAN, breathless and in panic.*)

BETHAN: The children, have you seen them?

PARCH: What children?
The year's dying, they grew.

BETHAN: John and Adela.
The master's house is empty. I went back,
Sara was there – but she wasn't!

PARCH: Hey, Ned Staner,
you making sense of this?

STANER: She got a stone,
Beth Coley, stone in her shoe, my lady.

BETHAN: A stone?

PARCH: Now she got green learning – 'estone, estone!'

WHITYARD: I saw the girl for sure –

BETHAN: You saw her – where?

WHITYARD: Up close, she was –

PARCH: He's dreaming in his drink,
you can't believe him.

WHITYARD: Silver she was and chuckled,
even as imagined by myself.

PARCH: See, he's in a meander.

BETHAN: Because there's a rider,
   a rider seen on the road, it's that I'm afraid of!
   They say it could be him, the murdering rider,
   hooded, he is, I heard at the barn, that rider,
   he leaves no man or woman alive –

STANER: Oh Tom,
   I heard that baron makes a pool of places,
   red like what with blood and that, you have to
   wade to church to see where the dead are hiding!

BETHAN: They ought to be in the house, I should have stayed there!
   Poor John, Adela, children in the winter!
   (*BETHAN runs off.*)

STANER: I'm for the moon, Tom Parch!

PARCH: And I clean over.
   Come on, reeve, you need a head on your shoulders
   to have this dream at all.

WHITYARD: Is it a nightmare?

PARCH: That's up to you, remember. The next chapter
   is all about discomfort and deep quiet.
   And him who sneezes sneezes out his soul.
   (*PARCH, STANER and WHITYARD hurry off. Enter JUXON,*
   better off than before. He sits and starts eating bread and fish.)

JUXON: Now there's a trick of oafs I do recall.
   I ought to thank 'em, seeing as how my shells
   have turned all into crowns since that hot day
   at Harvest, when those very dulberts told me
   I ought to swim to market.
   Ill-meant it were, but got me cogitatin'.
   Old East of England fair old weeps with rivers,
   and if I got me a boat and I could float it,
   I'd come to market sooner like. These days
   my trade is all of Norfolk, Suffolk, and some
   half the ways to Lincoln and to London.
   And here's the place where my good fortune grew,
   when I was warm and poorer. Younger, too.
   (*Enter the GIRL. He doesn't recognize her.*)
   Good evening to you there. I say hello there.

Now here's the quietest sentinel. A ghost?
Phantom or friend? I'll try the time-old test,
and tempt it with the Feast of the Leftover,
the dead being not so hungry, or not hungry
for a melch of herring on brown loaf.
I's wonderin' if you'd care for –
(*She snatches food from him and eats.*)
                                        Very human,
with manners of the South. I do salute you.
I'm a dulbert here. Or I'm no dulbert,
but bein' as I'm from somewhere far away,
I find it pays to play the part of dulbert.
You too seem an extranean round here.
Though, now I catch your eye, I wonder whether
I'm wholly an extranean to you…
There's something in the glow a mite too yellow –
If ever there's a light to render skin
a Lincoln green, then you I've seen before.
GIRL: From somewhere far away you are. How far?
JUXON: Ho now, thataway, some days and more,
    depending on the marshes and the markets,
    each as treacly treacherous as the other.
    Lynn's my kingdom. Up there by the sea.
GIRL: Up there by the sea.
    Home is by the sea, but home is here
    is poisont and forget me. Is my brother
    home? Is my brother home?
JUXON: You must be cold
    as the hull o'my craft, so shrug this on, little stranger,
    make a tradesman warm for doing a deal
    that got him nothing.
    (*JUXON gives the GIRL his overcoat.*)
GIRL: Poor old year forget me.
JUXON: Forget you? Ho, some chance.
    Some more of my old bread? I'll only eat it.
GIRL: Our…Faser…who art…is gone, is gone now.
JUXON: In Heaven, I think He is, and then He's hallowed,
    but after that? Well, if He art He art,

and all the rest is a freight of fine detail.
He art in an Englishman,
He art in a lost little soul and in its chatter,
whatever it means. Now, let's share. I believe
I owe you for a quarter-year of fortune,
dating from the day I thought I seen you.

GIRL: Is a salt food you af, is from the sea.

JUXON: For sure it is. Here now. It makes a change
to give away, you know, but how I see it:
suppers and coats should pass about with freedom
among the all-alones.

(*The GIRL takes his hand, and brings him to the edge of the pit.*)
                  Creepy old ditch.
Seen all sorts, I figure. What's the matter?

GIRL: Home?

JUXON: Home? How's that?
(*The bells begin to chime midnight.*)

GIRL: Is song of stone!

JUXON: A mercy, someone's eyes...

GIRL: Is song of stone!

(*JUXON drops in the pit, and emerges with the body of the BOY.*)

GIRL: Is song of stone, cheru!

JUXON: Let's sit him down
and warm him up, he'll soon –
(*He realises the BOY is dead.*)
(*Quietly.*) Our Father who art in Heaven, hallowed –
God bless, and all, and so.

GIRL: Is my brother home?
Is song of stone. We come by song of stone
we tend our faser's cose and is remember
we hear is song of stone!

JUXON: The bells of Bury,
ringin' away the old, is all the noise is.
(*JUXON stats to wrap the BOY in his undercoat.*)

GIRL: Poor old year forget me. Is not home!
Home is where I see it! We are the children –

JUXON: The children of where, of what? poor little friend.

139

GIRL: We are the children of St Martins land.
    We hold him dear and sing him in our churches.
    (*To the BOY.*) All cold and poisont
JUXON: No, dear,
    home is where it's green and so, he's warm.
GIRL: Green. Where we are of, all thing is green.
    Field and river, cose and dogs is green.
    Poor old stone forget me. Take me home.
JUXON: Too cold to dig, and nothing by to dig with.
    I'll lie him in the rocks,
    cover him up with earth and the loose pebbles.
    (*JUXON buries the BOY in the pit.*)
    Juxon, here's a lonely little wonder
    no mate of yours is going to down his ale
    and half-believe.
    (*Enter CALNE, who runs to the GIRL.*)
CALNE: Adela! Cold, I lost you!
    Where did you run to?
GIRL: Home we are not home.
    Avaci maru ur nay, ur nekh –
CALNE: Stop that,
    it's over, I'm here, it's Richard –
GIRL: Is forget me.
CALNE: And what might you be, sir?
JUXON: I might be this,
    a coatless man on a journey.
CALNE: Has he hurt you,
    Adela? – what's your business on this land?
JUXON: On England? Staying alive. On your dead field?
    Old fish and conversation.
CALNE: (*To the GIRL.*) Why are you wearing
    a stranger's coat?
JUXON: It isn't strange to him
    whose coat it was. And as for why she wears it,
    enquire you could of why the sun goes down
    and shivers us together.
CALNE: You have no right
    to linger in Woolpit, sir, these are the fields

of Bury St Edmund Abbey. What you breathe
is not your own.

JUXON: What you say's not *your* own,
 I judge by your red temper, sir, but truly,
 I'll pack and pass along if the Very St Edmund
 has had his fill of herring.

CALNE: What did you do?
 This girl, she is my business, my possession,
 my property – I'm a soldier of King Stephen!
 Answer me this instant!

JUXON: Holy nothing
 but munch and wonder. Shame she's your possession,
 for it's for far away she's got a yearning,
 and no word of a soldier.

CALNE: You're a liar!
 I want you off the Land and Liberty
 of Bury by first light, sir, otherwise
 you'll break a bloodhound's fast.

JUXON: I beg to differ.
 The cats'll have me first, on account of the herring.
 I'll walk until you're further off from me
 than I from you, and then I'm satisfied.
 (*Exit JUXON.*)

GIRL: He gone is by the sea?

CALNE: He's gone, Adela,
 forget the wretch.

GIRL: Is kingdom by the see-sigh.

CALNE: Why did you run away?

GIRL: Is a white is man who
 laugh and say is angels –

CALNE: I didn't laugh,
 I said, or was about to say, I – love you,
 do you understand?

GIRL: (*With disgust.*) Issa gahee ur nekh,
 Ur nekh, ur rookh, ur rassin –

CALNE: That ugly tongue
 is dead, do you hear?

GIRL: I love who.

CALNE: Look at me –

GIRL: Love who, lovhu, lovulavulavu
lafulafulafoolafool a fool –

CALNE: *Be quiet!*

GIRL: Someone is coming.

(*CALNE looks. The GIRL crawls to the edge of the pit, and won't move.*)

CALNE: A rider, we have to go...
Get up, come on, we were warned –

GIRL: Forget the wretch.

CALNE: Get up, I tell you, come on, there's danger now,
he's barely human –

GIRL: Why did he ran away...

CALNE: Get up, Adela, we have to hide, I can save you
but only if you let me –

GIRL: Let the rest,
forget the wretch a fool is ugly tongue
is green is danger hide we aff to save you
is barely your man ugly danger.

CALNE: Adela!

GIRL: Ur nekh, ur rookh, ur rassin.

CALNE: I can't fight him.
You understand? I have to run. I have to –
come with me, will you –

GIRL: Are my two arms yellow.
Hope me my two arms is by is sea now.

CALNE: Hope? If you don't need me then you have none.

(*CALNE flees. The GIRL sings.*)

GIRL: (*Sings.*) *The apples eat the year is die*
The sonn is clime in oversigh
The rob is flow the oh she why

(*Enter a RIDER, masked and hooded.*)

You come from far away?

You come from where is home?

You take me home with you now?

(*The RIDER nods. She goes to him. He pushes her down and tears her clothes. CALNE runs in and kills the RIDER with his sword. Commotion. The VILLAGERS arrive.*)

CALNE: You saw, did you, what he did?

PARCH: Well, it weren't much.
   You saw to that, Saint George.
CALNE: A hundred villages
   will thank me for it.
PARCH: What does a monster look like?
   Is anyone going to look? I'm not, myself,
   but some may be interested.
CALNE: I'm not afraid.
   I've shown I wasn't afraid.
SARA: You weren't afraid,
   Master, you were straight and true.
CALNE: I had to –
   I had to be.
   (*CALNE uncovers the face of the dead man. It is Parson*
   DEAZIL.)
BETHAN: Oh terrible, the parson!
STANER: Tom, it's the parson, look!
PARCH: I know the parson.
   It's yesterday for him and no mistake.
SARA: But we did see what he did.
PARCH: Or tried to do.
   Soldier put a stop to that.
SARA: I mean,
   an awful crime indeed, to overwhelm
   the little amber mite, who, after all,
   has given us such pleasure here.
PARCH: Oh well,
   I'm sure they'll understand, the monks at Bury,
   Master Calne, you did as you had to,
   him trying to have her and all. But it takes two.
SARA: Three if you count the reeve and Tom's a fourth.
BETHAN: But none of this is right, she wouldn't do that,
   she's just a child –
PARCH: How do you know, Beth Coley?
   You missed her in the darkness and she grew
   like weeds you didn't know of. Now we find her,
   habitual, she is, you'd have to say,
   and random in her favours.

CALNE: Is this true?

SARA: Perhaps it was only you who was strong enough
to overcome temptation, Master Richard,
presuming that you did.

CALNE: How can you doubt it?
A rotted thing like that.

SARA: But I don't doubt it.
I know you much too well.

WHITYARD: We killed the parson.
It's not a dream. They'll hang us all.

CALNE: Be quiet.
We struck in error.

PARCH: *We* didn't strike at all.

CALNE: We'll bury him. Nobody knows he came,
he's – look, he wore a mask and hood. He meant
evil business here, and met his ending.
Nobody saw anything. We six,
understand?

SARA: And what of our rosy seventh?

STANER: Rosy, she is, like anything that's going.
She's not no other colour.

SARA: Green with hatred,
green with hunger, she was, if she was ever,
well now she's had 'em all, she could be Sara.

BETHAN: Where did your brother go?

SARA: I saw him running,
running away.

STANER: Me too, he was laughing at us!

CALNE: Dig in the pit, you three, while the air's blue
and no one's yet about.

PARCH: Ahem. Ahem.
Tell him, reeve, our agreement.

STANER: This is the year
we not got ever to work!

CALNE: What's this nonsense?

WHITYARD: It's simple to tell you. Parch and Staner here,
I promised them a year's respite of labour,
beginning with this morning.

144

CALNE: Why did you do that?

WHITYARD: They asked me in my dream. I did it gladly,
    knowing as I'd wake up one fine morning.

CALNE: Dig. Head down and dig.

    (*PARCH, STANER and WHITYARD pull the body into the*
    pit, and dig. The GIRL becomes agitated.)

CALNE: What's wrong? Be quiet.
    You brought this madness on us, so we'll stow him
    where we want, we'll stow him in your pit,
    unloving urchin wretch.

WHITYARD: I've found a coat,
    but it's all full of stones.

CALNE: Head down and dig.
    Bethan, take her back to the house. Believe me,
    she won't get out again. Sara, Bethan,
    tie her down if you have to. This is the last
    noise she'll make out here. Dig, dig fast.

Act Four: Spring

Scene One

Spring, the Wolfpit. Strange flowers have appeared.

SONG

She said the violets never flower
  Upon her window-ledge,
She said the crocuses would wither
  Round her garden's edge.
She said I was her Valentine
I said, 'Was I?' She wasn't mine
  So Ladysmock and Cuckoo Pint
  And Jill-go-by-the-hedge.

Ladysmock is soft and pink
  Upon her window-ledge,
But see the throbbing Cuckoo Pint
  About the forest edge.
She asked me pick the Pint for her,
I said I had one, she said, 'Where?'
  So Ladysmock and Cuckoo Pint
  And Jill-go-by-the-hedge.

The evening's long and light again
  Outside the window-ledge
And midges merge and spiders spin
  Around the meadow edge,
I went with her as far as this,
But don't you ask how far that is,
I'll take it out and point and piss
  On Ladysmock and Cuckoo Pint
  And Jill-go-by-the-hedge.

Jills, your Jacks are walking by
  Below your window-ledge.
And sigh and breathe and breathe and sigh
  About your garden's edge.

And breathe and sigh and blow and suck
And lick their lips and try their luck
So ask them up to pick and pluck
The Ladysmock and Cuckoo Pint
And Jill-go-by-the-hedge.

(*PARCH and STANER see the clump of strange flowers.*)

STANER: Now look, Tom – see? It wasn't in my mind.

PARCH: That I know, I know your mind for a region
    forty days and nights a man may roam
    without a shrub for company.

STANER: But Tom,
    Tom Parch, it ain't one shrub, it's many flowers.

PARCH: Well pinch me in the winter, Ned. You breathe,
    warm air, that is, we call it 'spring', we do,
    hereabouts. You call it what you care to.

STANER: Not daffodils, Tom Parch, nor marigolds
    nor crocuses.

PARCH: Or hollyhocks or beans.
    We'll pass the day just so. I'll show you things,
    and you apprise me of the things they're not.
    Else, sure, I'll pick a dog or stroke a daisy.

STANER: These flowers have happened here –

PARCH: Have happened where?
    Where nothing happened, Ned.

STANER: Where nothing grows.
    Nothing grows all year nor yesterday,
    I know, on account of how I came by here
    once in a wander, Tom.

PARCH: A wander. It's nothing,
    nothing but spring, when Nature's like the young,
    playing a prank before she's old enough
    to think how it's not funny. And it's not.
    She knows it's not but blushes and persists.
    She'll wind up in a rosy sulk.

STANER: Tom Parch…

PARCH: A further bloom in the brain?

STANER: A greenish bloom.
    What if –

PARCH: What if? What if?
   Women with four heads which disagree
   are Queens of the Republic of What-If.
   There's no what-if in Suffolk nor in England.
   This is the holy Kingdom of So-What,
   and you're a trespasser.

STANER: No that I'm not.
   But see one coming, Tom – we better pretend
   we got some business here. – Like I was saying,
   Tom, I'll pay you seven crowns –
   (Enter JUXON, whom they don't recognise in daylight.)

JUXON: For what?

STANER: Excuse us, stranger, we've some business here.

JUXON: Oh, don't mind me, I'm quite extranean
   to your transaction. I'm a Norfolk man,
   I haunt old haunts. Seven crowns for what?
   I'm curious.

STANER: You should be curious. Tom,
   he should be curious, shouldn't he?

PARCH: Not ever.
   This ain't no stranger's business.

STANER: For the – flowers!
   I'll pay you seven crowns for –

PARCH: Shut up, Ned,
   more than enough what-if and let's-pretend.

JUXON: Seven crowns for these? Perplexing flowers.
   They pepper this good mood with little seeds
   of questions.

PARCH: Let me peck them from your world.
   They're mine, he's paying seven crowns for one.

STANER: *(To PARCH.)*
   Not each, Tom Parch, that's seven crowns the lot.

PARCH: *(To STANER.)*
   It's let's-pretend, I'm pretending it's each one.

STANER: *(To PARCH.)*
   It's let's-pretend, I'm pretendin' that it's not!

JUXON: I see you've got some business here. I'll sit,
   I'll sit and sigh, and envy you your flowers.

STANER: You shouldn't do that, stranger.

JUXON: Why's that?

STANER: It's cursed round here. We call these flowers 'curse-flowers'!
    And Jill-go-by – no, Sara-go-by-the-hedge.

JUXON: Sara-go-by-the-hedge. A fair name, Sara.

STANER: It isn't. Why's that so? How do you know that?

PARCH: Something's knocking, Ned. You ever been here
    formerly, John Norfolk?

JUXON: Been here?
    I never in my life passed by in daylight,
    and, if I did, I saw no human man,
    nor human woman, sir, no, nothing human.
    (*JUXON produces a bag of money and starts counting out golden
    coins.*)

PARCH: Try not to blink, we'll lose 'em if we blink.

JUXON: Forty crowns for seven of your curse-flowers,
    Master businessman, I am that taken.

PARCH: Forty crowns?

STANER: I'll do the countin', Tom.

PARCH: Count sparrows, Ned. I'll take it. Let me pick 'em!

JUXON: Don't pick 'em, sir, I say you leave 'em be.
    I'll buy the plot off you.

STANER: What, Suffolk ground?

JUXON: Dig it, it don't mind.

STANER: No, no, don't dig it!

JUXON: Good, we'll leave the flowers to rest in peace,
    and that one, those and them two I will have.

PARCH: Good choices, sir, if I may say so. Now,
    forty crowns, you said?
    (*JUXON pays PARCH.*)

PARCH: And forty nights.

STANER: Good choices, aren't they, Tom? That's twenty crowns
    me and twenty you.

PARCH: Not wholly, Ned.
    I was the salesman in the let's-pretend.

STANER: But them's real forty crowns!

PARCH: Consider yourself
    friend of a real friend, thus fortunate.

STANER: (*To JUXON.*) He's bammin' with me, sir, he always does it,
    no hurt he means.
PARCH: You off now, then – sir?
JUXON: Reckon I'll lag a while, and not so far
    I can't inhale the air of my seven blooms.
STANER: He won't inhale the others, will he, Tom,
    'cause that's more crowns.
JUXON: I think I see more colours,
    and not at all curse-flowers.
    (*Enter SARA and BETHAN.*)
SARA: My, and Edmond Staner told a tale
    that spilt and settled true. What are these weeds?
STANER: Weeds? They're flowers, Sara,
    and each is seven crowns, and me and Tom,
    we sold 'em to the Norfolk man hereby.
    Forty crowns we got, Tom's got 'em now,
    he's treasurer.
PARCH: I'm treasuring 'em, Ned.
BETHAN: You bought these flowers, sir?
JUXON: The seven, lady.
SARA: If you don't pick 'em, I will.
PARCH: Steady, Sara,
    the man's half built of crowns.
SARA: To hell with money.
    This is our land, and this is our – our wasteland.
STANER: Where nothing happened, Sara.
JUXON: Go by the hedge.
SARA: What did you say? – I know,
    I know who planted these. You root them up,
    you'll see there's nothing under. I know who,
    and when, and why.
BETHAN: Why would she do that, Sara?
    She doesn't know her mind.
SARA: I know her mind.
    (*SARA starts picking the flowers. Enter WHITYARD.*)
WHITYARD: You stop your picking of the Master's flowers!
SARA: I've stopped and they're not flowers.
JUXON: And not the master's.

WHITYARD: I have been duly notified of these
    unusualities growing, and I'm here
    to see them for myself, and by thus seeing
    do see for the Master.

BETHAN: They're the stranger's flowers.
    Tom sold him seven, seven crowns a stem.

PARCH: Oh tell the bees and butterflies, why not.

WHITYARD: Doubly, doubly strange. Who is this fellow?

JUXON: I'm even stranger, friend. I have a spade
    beside the stream nearby. I'll dig my flowers
    out of the earth and walk.

PARCH / STANER: No you can't dig!

WHITYARD: You can't dig, sir, they'll be no digging here.

SARA: What's all this din and digging? We all know
    who dreamed this up.

WHITYARD: Dreamed it up, you say?
    Too rich a yellow for a dreaming up.
    Nobody dreams that yellow.

JUXON: Well I might have to,
    seeing as I can't dig, and I can't go,
    so do my flowers hold me here, I ought to
    sleep to pass the time.

STANER: No you can't sleep!

JUXON: Can't sleep, can't dig, can't go. Would you like a song?
    (*Sings.*) *Hickamore-ackamore, sitteth over the kitchen door...*

WHITYARD: That won't be necessary, here's our master
    to organise what's next.
    (*Enter CALNE.*)

CALNE: What is this huddle?
    Master Whityard, I wanted this cleared up.

WHITYARD: The complicating all is this man's doing,
    who claims he bought the blossoms of Tom Parch,
    and won't move on, because,
    because he's not allowed to dig. Is he?

CALNE: Who is this vagabond?

JUXON: You don't know me.

CALNE: I've never met you.

JUXON: No. But you don't know me.

CALNE: A riddler. Weed this bank,
    Bethan, Sara, Ned. And you be gone.
    You must be from the realm of upside down
    to waste your gold on weeds, and to this man,
    this evident old fraud. Clear the bank.
JUXON: You want assistance, friends? The roots are deep,
    we have to dig –
PARCH: You linger here with me, sir.
    (*PARCH hauls JUXON out of the way, as the VILLAGERS
    begin pulling out the flowers. Enter the GIRL, white, hair
    cropped short. JUXON doesn't recognise her at first.*)
PARCH: Who whistled her this way?
GIRL: I heard them say of flowers fresh on the pit.
    I come to see it only.
CALNE: No flowers now.
    I let you out to work, not to sniff flowers.
SARA: Come to see it, she says – we know you did it.
GIRL: Did it? Sara, what?
STANER: Be quiet, Sara,
    The Norfolk fellow's lingering.
GIRL: (*Seeing JUXON.*)   Here's you.
JUXON: Here's me. I don't know you, but yes, here's me,
    and now here's me, and soon there's me, and so
    I take my leave of Woolpit forty crowns
    the poorer, seven weeds a richer man.
    (*BETHAN gives JUXON the seven cut flowers.*)
BETHAN: Here you are.
JUXON: I thank you for the dead.
CALNE: Take your trophies, eat them when you're hungry.
    There's nothing here for you.
PARCH: Unless you'd pay
    a crown for a moon-story?
STANER: Let him go, Tom Parch, let him go away,
    we got the forty crowns.
PARCH: He parts with that
    For seven weeds a week from his own home,
    he must be ranking rich.
CALNE: What's your mischief,
    Parch?

PARCH: It's business merely, Master Richard,
 excusing me. – Now sir, we boast at Woolpit
 two marvels, one a sight to see, and one
 a yarn to hear. You've seen our flowers that grow
 where nothing does? Now, for a slender crown,
 you'll hear the Tale of Martinstown from One
 Who Knows…

WHITYARD: Not that again. We hear this moonshine
 every day.

SARA: Nor never meant a thing.

STANER: But him, he's never heard it, Sara! I like
 Tom's latest plan!

WHITYARD: The tale's a fantasy.

STANER: It's funny though!

BETHAN: It's only a lost child
 mumbling what she heard.

SARA: And so we pay her,
 we serve her right for trying her luck with us,
 the little stoat.

CALNE: I can't spare her all day
 for you to have your witless pleasure. I need
 the fire laid, the floor washed.

SARA: (*To JUXON.*) You listen,
 sir, you'll pay a crown for every chuckle.

GIRL: Poor old year forget me.

STANER: Hear it, sir?
 She thinks it's New Year's Night instead of…
 whatever it is.

JUXON: Why pay for Suffolk yarns?
 You know me for a Norfolk man. Where I am
 we ride to church on dragons.

PARCH: Sir, be patient,
 you see her eyes? She quite believes it all.

JUXON: I see her eyes.

GIRL: Poor old year forget me.

SARA: Tell him, frog-princess, where is your home?

PARCH: A crown each time you laugh.

JUXON: Well, I accept.

153

STANER: A crown to me and Tom each time you laugh.
JUXON: And six if I believe.
SARA: Don't hold your breath.
    Go on, get her croaking.
PARCH: Sit you down,
    Norfolk man and listen to these marvels.
    Where do you come from, girl?
GIRL: I am the children of St Martins Land.
PARCH: 'Children,' she goes, on account she had a brother.
    We don't know where he went. We think he went
    to tell it to the Empress! How d'you hold him?
GIRL: I hold him dear and sing him in my churches.
    All my land is green, the sky is green –
STANER: This is a good part, green she's saying!
JUXON: I heard her.
STANER: Did he laugh, Tom?
PARCH: He almost did, he's cracking!
GIRL: The air and trees and cows are green. One day
    I were…and with my brother in my field
    and with my father's cows…
JUXON: And is he green,
    your father?
GIRL: He is green, my father.
PARCH: A crown?
    He laughed.
JUXON: No, I believed.
PARCH: Six of 'em then.
GIRL: We hear a song of bells, is like the bells
    at Bury, and we follow,
    we follow to a – cave and is for ever
    long and dark and in the end is light,
    yellow light as nothing in the world is,
    and so we come to you and in your England
    where you is reaping blood and so you find us.
    We try but never find a road away.
    I love you, you have save me.   (*Parch.*)
    I love you, you have teach me.   (*Sara.*)
    I love you, you have love me.   (*Calne.*)

STANER: I always laugh at that!

JUXON: I'm not surprised.
What with all that love.

SARA: St Martins Land.
Tell us about your stretch of Suffolk, dear…

BETHAN: She doesn't know, she's lost it, sir –

PARCH: Shut up!
Look at his eyes, all brimming up with silver
so much he credits her! The light, Adela!

GIRL: Adela live by a light…but, but only…
But only light as is it not a darkness.
And where we are is all light ever so,
as in an East when night is at his end,
as in a West when day is.
But over a broad river, far away,
there is a land is always brightly shines,
and so we look and say is land of Jesus.

CALNE: You've had your fun. This fellow disbelieves
and didn't laugh. Adela, home.

GIRL: My home.
Sea-sigh and he forget me, land of Jesus.

CALNE: Home. *Now.*

JUXON: Home, unhappy creature,
back where you belong, and where that is,
I hope is where I am.

CALNE: What did you say?

JUXON: I don't believe I care to tell you, sir.

PARCH: I don't believe we care what you don't believe.

JUXON: Then I'll say I hope she might belong with me.
(*To the GIRL.*) I don't forget you. I remember you,
another face and season. We were sharing,
a supper by the pit.

GIRL: Is Somartang.
You are from by the sea.

PARCH: Who is this waster?

STANER: He's smiling at her, Tom, he owes us money!

PARCH: Pay me for your tears of laughter!

STANER: Pay him!

JUXON: Shut your mouth, or I will belk you, sir,
    from here to the Hook of Holland.
    (*To the GIRL.*) I know you, and I ask you will you come
    away from here, to Lynn, up by the sea?
GIRL: Is all I want.
CALNE: Hell's teeth at what you want,
    or what he wants – I want this idiot gone,
    and you upon your knees on my stone floor!
    I am the master here.
JUXON: You're nothing here.
    You are outside the law.
CALNE: So help me God – hold him, I'll kill the wretch!
JUXON: Kill me, kill who you like, nothing will spring
    the gentleman from where he's buried, sir,
    with neither cross nor stone.
    Before you kill me, look to the forest edge,
    and see my brothers watching from the trees.
    They bar all ways from Woolpit to the far
    points of Suffolk shire, and they all know
    the bones of what I saw that winter night.
    It doesn't ask my bones nor his to peddle
    stories at the Abbey, but it'll cost you
    more than crowns, and tears of something else.
    Leave her alone forever.
STANER: I'm leaving her.
SARA: She's ours, she is our servant, vagabond,
    she's Richard's property.
JUXON: I do not think
    she's even earth's, and as for what you think,
    young spitting thing, I hold not the least regard.
    (*JUXON scatters coins, and the VILLAGERS crawl about to
    gather them.*)
    Here's crowns for all forever, until the night
    this sleeping country sighs and throws you off
    her hot grey sheets. Then all you need are crowns
    for this eye and that eye. Here, little one,
    now we've nothing, nothing but a host
    of friends and brothers heading to the sea,

and then our pebble home on a pebble shore,
where the stones forever murmur. Say your goodbyes
to Woolpit, for it's gone, and history
will have it for a ditch that had a village.
(*Exit JUXON and the GIRL.*)

BETHAN: So sudden a goodbye – perhaps she doesn't
understand? I'll watch them to the stream.

WHITYARD: I'll go with you, Beth Coley, so I'm sure
it's all an end to dreaming. Now I'll sleep
with open eyes and always on my guard.
(*Exit BETHAN and WHITYARD.*)

SARA: Your stones will go unwashed, Master Richard.

CALNE: My stones? I'm leaving anyway. Tomorrow.
Today, I'm leaving now. I'm riding west.

SARA: West?

CALNE: To the war, of course.

PARCH: Oh, there's a war?
You riding for the Empress, or the King?

CALNE: For the war. For anyone. Anything.
(*Exit CALNE.*)

SARA: There goes a brave man nowhere, or a coward
somewhere, either way a man who fits.

STANER: Look, I can still see 'em,
vagabond and her. They met their folk,
them greeting her, she smiles – if I was a Norfolk
it's this back they'd be slapping.

SARA: Shut your eyes,
idiot, so Norfolk buys a slattern
off of the Suffolk: so?

STANER: I only mean –
I only mean she once was what she was.

SARA: Was she? Was she? All I can remember
are words that didn't mean, and a wild story
so black it took a Northman to believe it.
I don't remember anything I believed.

STANER: Do you remember, Tom, the day we found 'em?
(*PARCH is counting crowns.*)

PARCH: That's seven and seventy crowns, and plus my fourth,

that's –
STANER: I'll do it –
SARA: One hundred seventeen.
   (*Exit SARA.*)
STANER: I got a load too, Tom.
PARCH: So buy some flowers.
   Today I'll quite forget. It's crowns as do it.
   Good luck to him with her. It's a fine riddance.
   One hundred seventeen and all forgot.
   You coming for some hours of ale, Ned Staner?
   Spring day like this.
STANER: Not this once, old Tom.
   I think I'll – walk, and, like you said, not think,
   but just be here and there, and hear the birds,
   and see all Suffolk things, and say some only-
   I-can-hear-'em words.
   (*Exit STANER.*)
PARCH: Suit yourself. He always suits himself.
   One hundred seventeen and all forgot.
   That's forgot, but me, I'm not forgot.
   I'll be the man who found 'em in the tale,
   the Tale, it'll be, of Tom.
   I found 'em as God made 'em, if God made 'em.
   He did, He made 'em. I was chose to find 'em.
   And so I did, just here. But that's forgot.
   That's forgot, but I won't be forgot.
   My deeds'll be passed down, as like as not.
   I'll pass 'em down some day. The Many Tales
   of Tom the Workman. Now. Apples and ales
   till all the fellows come. Apples and ales.

THE ONLY GIRL IN THE WORLD

A Play of Jack the Ripper

Characters

JOSEPH BARNETT
30, a foreman at Billingsgate fish market,
a Londoner

MARY JANE KELLY
23, an immigrant, fair / ginger hair,
Irish-Welsh background, soft Welsh accent

The action takes place in Whitechapel, 1888.

Note: A third actor can profitably be used, as a musician, as the shape in the bed that Mary says is 'Mrs Van Turney', as Mary's last 'gentleman', or anything else that's required.

This play was first performed in July 2001 at Hoxton Hall, London with the following cast:

JOE, David Peacock
MARY, Rebecca Adamson
ACCORDIONIST, Bob Karper

Director, Robert Horwell
Designer, Chloe Pettit
Produced by Melanie Sykes for Volition.

Act One

Scene One

Commercial Street.

(*JOE knocks off work, Saturday afternoon.*)

JOE: And that's the last, or else I'm some machine.
    I'll see you lads on Monday. What do you mean
    where's Joe think he's heading? Nothing more
    I'd like than slap these fish around all weekend
    just for fun, mind you, it's not the money,
    nothing more. You see me of a Sunday,
    squatting here among 'em, I'm the priest
    of all the blinkin' haddock.
    (*MARY loitering.*)

MARY: Well I never.
    They told me here's a place I might go fishing.
    I said all right, I didn't know they're meaning
    souls half man, half fish.

JOE: I beg your pardon,
    my language was – my language was –

MARY: Don't tell me,
    Cod Latin.

JOE: No, madame, ill-treated English,
    begging your pardon –

MARY: Don't beg on your knees, mate,
    you'll slide away in fishblood.

JOE: We've a boy
    who swabs the place.

MARY: He does? What, once a year?
    I thought my dream came true when I smelt fish.

JOE: I beg your pardon?

MARY: You don't seem to do much
    save begging. What are you, a dogfish?

JOE: I'm
    wondering if you're, madame, in some

    form or other, taking me for someone
    other, as it were, mistakingly,
    namely, for my workmates?
MARY: (No, you'll do.)
    How do you breathe in this job?
JOE: What's that?
MARY: Beg my pardon. Where's your North Sea manners?
    You take me for a fishwife?
JOE: Beg your pardon,
    I'm on my half-day.
MARY: Seeing how the sunshine's
    sloping off I'd say the whole of London's
    on a half-day. Better get to work, eh?
JOE: Home from work, you mean? I'm off to bed.
MARY: To bed, to work, we're talking the same Latin.
    What do you need?
JOE: What do I need?
MARY: They told me
    you fish boys got a bonus what with all
    your Russian ships came in?
JOE: We did indeed.
    Safe in the bank, I stowed it.
MARY: That's a pity.
    I had a savings scheme, I could have helped you.
    You clean, then, you been swabbed?
JOE: I'm not, I'm not, madame,
    entirely sure what business you and I
    could be transacting of. Name's Joseph Barnett,
    foreman of Billingsgate, as of this very,
    yesterday, it were. I bought my hat
    direct I were about this morning.
MARY: Ah...
    You work in fish. Funny, it hadn't dawned.
JOE: Foreman, though, not porter, as of lately.
    Tell me by my apron!
MARY: Well of course,
    if you're as quick as Joe, you can. Myself,
    I'm with the House of Lords, but you knew that.

JOE: You like a joke, don't you?

MARY: It seems that way.
I reckon we're transacted out then, Joseph,
the half-day's turning quarter-day.

JOE: Joe, call me.

MARY: Why? We'll never meet again. I ain't
swimming by your dock again in this life.

JOE: That's sad to hear.

MARY: Why would I?
It's not as if I've time on my hands.

JOE: Your hands look c-cold.

MARY: They're always this c-colour.
Take a cold last look, and kick for shore.

JOE: I don't know what's your line, madame, so I don't
rightly know the answer to the question
why you'd never come again, but it's sad,
sometimes, to think of things that only happen
once and all, then...

MARY: Never.

JOE: As y'say there.
What was your name?

MARY: What *was* it? What am I dead?

JOE: Well, yes, if you say *never* and it's true
we never meet again. Are your hands frozen?

MARY: Why are my hands your business on a half-day?
Yes, I lost my gloves. But that don't matter,
I stowed them in the bank.

JOE: I got new gloves, though,
along with my new titfer. I could spare them.

MARY: That's not – I'm sorry, squire, but you're not quite
what I expected here. I think my hands
are happy freezing, ain'tcha. What *was* my name?
If you was a carpenter you'd have it straight.

JOE: I would?

MARY: That's it, Joe, woodwork,
I'd tell you by your apron. You'd be Joseph,
a carpenter, and I'd be? I'd be?
We'd wander through the desert, with a star
for company, you getting there? Jesus...

JOE: But you see I'm not a c-c-carpenter –
MARY: Just as well
    if you can't say the word. Reckon you're not
    a collier, then, and not a cardinal.
    It's Mary, for my sins. You're a f-f-fish man.
JOE: Mary, that's a fine name.
MARY: Don't go by it
    lately, I'm Marie, Marie-Jeanette,
    à la parisienne, à la mademoiselle.
JOE: Mad-moselle, mad-moselle Marie then.
MARY: Got any other qu-qu-questions?
JOE: Well yes, many indeed, but they're like fish
    the way they're slipping out.
MARY: So *you* need gloves,
    not me, then you can hold things.
JOE: I must insist
    you take these gloves from me.
MARY: No, get lost.
    What do you think I am? Oh, I forgot,
    you've not the dimmest notion. When you never
    see me again you will still see my hands,
    and they may wave, just like Victoria's,
    only lifelike. About this time tomorrow
    they'll be around a beer-glass in the Ringers
    on Dorset Street. Myself, I'll be elsewhere,
    and won't know you for dust. It's just, this way,
    it's your fault if it's never.
    (*She goes.*)
JOE: Mad-moselle,
    count on me to be there, if I may be.
    Tomorrow's my whole day, my holiday!
    See me for dust, you boys, I'm headed home!
    You saw her? What's so funny? That's Marie,
    that is, Marie-Jeanette, the little blighters.
    The mystery mad-moselle...

Scene Two

The Ringers Pub.

JOE: Got the time, mate, have you?
    Nearly three? that's longer than a day.
    I will have a bitter… Oh, I'll have a Burtons.
    You sure you haven't seen her, name Marie,
    or Mary, sure, there's Marys by the sack-load,
    what with the Irish. Red hair, you remember?
    Yeah, in a dress – you're having fun with me!
    No further questions, then.
    (*MARY arrives.*)
MARY: You didn't say 'a famed society beauty',
    so how is he to know?
JOE: Good day again,
    Marie Jeanette.
MARY: They call me Ginger here.
    That's what you should have said.
    At the Ten Bells it's Blue-eyes. Have I blue eyes?
JOE: More green than blue.
MARY: Oh really? I can't see.
JOE: They're eggshell-green.
MARY: You ate some funny eggs,
    mate. Remind me never to eat breakfast
    anywhere near you. Some chance of that.
    Not of the early risers, as it happens.
    'A beer, Ginger?' 'Yes please, Mr Eggshells.'
    What's your name again?
JOE: It's Joe Barnett,
    Joe, Joe with the gloves.
MARY: They all have gloves.
JOE: A beer, please, for Mary Jeannette, for Ginger!
    Now you've got gloves, I see.
MARY: You don't miss much.
JOE: I pride myself on observations.
MARY: Truly,
    I noticed that.

JOE: So, here's another one.
  You – are not from round here.
MARY: O wir?
  Na glyfar ohonoch chi, syr.
JOE: Further proof
  if any were required!
MARY: You fish-magician,
  Joseph Barnett.
JOE: Which of the Irish regions
  hail you from, as it were?
MARY: East Gingerland.
  And now I'm from Thrawl Street, like anyone
  who's no one.
JOE: Your good health.
  I live nearby, the same, I mean, like you do.
  George Street.
MARY: That ain't nearby.
  George Street's some other world. George Street's the moon.
JOE: Well, I'm the man in it!
MARY: That's pretty handy.
  Always did want to go there. What you got,
  one of them air balloons? We going to float there?
JOE: Well…you want to see it, see my place
  of habitat?
MARY: It's quite a choice to make,
  isn't it, Joe Barnett? Either that,
  or round to mine, step over the ghost children,
  go by the lass with half a face, turn right
  at the dog that died this morning and we're home.

                    (Joe's lodgings.)

JOE: Humble abode.
MARY: `That's magic, Joe, that is.
  'Humble abode,' he goes.
  When he has things like curtains, and a carpet.
  Know what I use for curtains? I'm not saying.
  Where does this lead to, Joe?
JOE: It's a little k-kitchen.
MARY: Whose little k-kitchen?

JOE: Mine, mine own.

MARY: That's yours and all? You been to C-California,
    Joe, got gold dust under them nails?

JOE: Don't think so!

MARY: But you've no bed. You sleep with your fellow fishies?
    (*JOE is moving her things in.*)

JOE: By all means I've a bed, in the next room,
    and a fire too, three chairs.

MARY: Joseph, Mary,
    and *Jeezus...*

JOE: This I call my parlour room.

MARY: Me parlour room, by George.

JOE: Here's all your things.

MARY: They're not my only things. I have a friend
    she's keeping stuff up West.

JOE: You lived up West?

MARY: I lived up West for sure. I had a life
    like nothing you could figure from a look.
    Silk curtains and soft carpets. Happens, Joseph.
    Every hour you know me you'll find out
    I did more things and went more places. Soon
    you'll stagger under lives I led before you.

JOE: I too, you will discover,
    in time, have been a man, or gentleman,
    of business, of affairs.

MARY: This thing needs dusting.

JOE: I'll leave these here for now.

MARY: You excellent
    new foreman of fish matters.

JOE: Well, it's knowing
    how to stack and load does come in handy.

MARY: I am convinced it does. Those are my dresses.
    Do you want to see them, Joseph?

JOE: Well indeed
    out of a c-c-curiosity –

MARY: Your tongue
    won't let you think your thought, you've got a right
    Church of England tongue there.

JOE: I indeed
    have certain –
MARY: Mine they tell me's Holy Roman.
    It finds a dark place, tattles and is sorry.
JOE: A dark place?
MARY: For confession, Joseph Barnett.
JOE: C-c-c-
MARY: See, it's all heretical
    to you. I'll reunite our broken faiths,
    crowd up the place with Catholics!
    (*MARY starts throwing the dresses around the room and at JOE.*)
JOE: Marie,
    Marie!
MARY: Now come on, Joseph,
    we've found our little stable.
JOE: No, this way,
    Marie, not here.
MARY: Not here?
JOE: Them walking by
    they'll see us.
MARY: Sheeps and shepherds, goats and angels,
    Joe, you got no room?
JOE: I've got a room
    we'll never leave!
MARY: You have? Has it got space
    for new religions?
JOE: For your one, we've sufficient!
    (*They go out together.*)

Scene Three

The Music Hall. Friday night.

(*MARY a little drunk, and heckling.*)

MARY: Don't hush me,
    we paid, and we're the Barnetts!
JOE: It's all right.
MARY: It's not all right. She thinks it's Sunday school.

JOE: It's a grand night, Marie. You said the Barnetts
    like we were wedded!

MARY: Hear that, sunshine?
    It's a grand night, says Joe. You look at me
    like that he'll settle you. That girl they found
    in George Yard, that wasn't a gang murder,
    sunshine, she was giving me the eye
    when Joe was looking, wasn't she?

JOE: It's all right,
    let's watch the show. They got that Champagne Charlie
    on after next.

MARY: What do you mean, pipe down?
    Do we think we own the place, mate? But we do!
    We'll sling you out in no time, eh Joe?

Scene Four

Victoria Park. Sunday afternoon.

(*JOE has MARY's head in his lap. Her eyes are closed but she's awake.*)

JOE: You sleeping now, Marie? I like it here.
    Everybody does, you look.
    Everybody does. You're sleeping now.
    Marie Jeanette, ma share.
    I pawned my suit, my love. I shouldn't talk
    business style on Sunday, but we've got
    slight difficulties of financial natures.
    When I didn't know you, angel,
    (*MARY opens her eyes.*)
    I were saving, as I never
    did indulge in all grand things we do now,
    the Paragon, the pub at night, excursions…
    Our way of life, the way we go at things,
    it's grand but if you took,
    I don't know, some small work,
    small work, not all week, mind,
    piece-work, shoes or matches, shoes, or matches,

(*MARY closes her eyes.*)
Supplemental to my waged position…
Not vital, well, you know. You are my lady,
my one whose needs I, not by all means vital,
these darned monetary matters… Indeed, sleep now,
Miss Kelly, mademoisella…
(*Lights down, then up on the pub. MARY there singing; while
JOE is in the room, tidying. He fetches hot water, makes his tea,
and sits at the table, waiting.*)

Scene Five

The Alley / George Street.

MARY: (*Sings.*)   *Calon lan yn llawn daioni,*
             Tecach yw na'r lili dlos,
             'D oes ond calon lan all ganu
             Canu'r dydd a chanu'r nos.

Irish? Are you idiots? It's French.
It is, it's dialect, it's western French,
you ignoramuses. You look it up
in the ignoramus dictionary.
(*She walks back to the Alley. She hears something and stops.*)
Hello? Joe, are you there?
Somebody lost your way, no?
Morganstone – is that you? Morganstone?
Don't mess with me, love, not your little Janey.
Who is that? Shame on you.
This is my home, my husband's there, you know.
(*Inside.*)
Told him you were my husband.

JOE: So I heard.
Who's Morganstone? Wizard from Old Wales,
he sounds like.

MARY: Not a wizard, not from Wales.
Not anything to me.

JOE: Who's little Janey?

MARY: You never asked who I was talking to.
Some man was on my tail the whole way home.

JOE: From the pub, Marie? From the Ringers?

MARY: All the way from there, but I never saw him.
    Must be the one they're after for the Smith girl,
    they never saw him either.

JOE: Maybe not,
    maybe it's Morganstone, the Welsh magician.

MARY: Leave it, Joe, let be.

JOE: And his little Janey.

MARY: No such people. Joe. I lost my shawl.
    I left my shawl.

JOE: Marie, the landlord came.

MARY: He did, did he, he's scum.

JOE: May have to leave,
    Marie, what with our funds, end of the month.
    We've nothing for him, being he's not inclined
    to wait. And I been sat here,
    been sitting here, I should say,
    thinking.

MARY: I've been singing.
    That's you and me, my Joe, that's our two ways
    parting in a sentence.

JOE: Got my sister
    up on the Grays Inn Road, it's quite a slog,
    like miles for me, for work, I mean –

MARY: It's miles
    from home, Joe.

JOE: But it might *be* like home,
    given time.

MARY: I'm biding here.

JOE: Marie,
    we got no choice.

MARY: I'm going to do my thinking
    in bed, Mr Joe Barnett. I will weigh
    the matters whom…are on your mind, my sunshine,
    I mean moonlight, I mean cloudlight.

Scene Six

Billingsgate Fish Market / The Ringers Pub.

JOE: And that's the last, or else I'm some machine!
　　I'll see you, lads. I can't – I'm going down
　　my local, see my lady. Yes, that lady.
　　You better not be meaning what you're saying,
　　or you'll be down the dock-gates, my old son,
　　or kipping in the spike. Yeah, same to you…
　　(*JOE gets a newspaper and goes to the pub. MARY comes in.*)
　　My lady!
MARY:　　　Where? You mean…? Oh…
　　Good afternoon, monsieur.
JOE:　　　　　　　　　　She been in France,
　　Ginger, she's seen the world!
MARY:　　　　　　　　　　It's all there was.
　　Guess where *I* been, Joseph.
JOE: Working the streets? I'm joking!
MARY:　　　　　　　　　　Our new home.
JOE: We've not got a new home.
MARY:　　　　　　　　Speak for yourself.
　　The landlord came. I reckoned it was time
　　I told him what I thought, and that felt sweet,
　　you ought to try it. Anyway, the girls
　　came by and helped me carry things.
JOE:　　　　　　　　　　　　What girls?
MARY: Sal, you know, and Lizzie, the blonde girls.
JOE: I know the word for what they are.
MARY:　　　　　　　　　　　They're blonde,
　　sunshine, from the country of the blonde.
JOE: The word for what they really are, a word
　　we don't use any more.
MARY:　　　　　　　I found a place!
JOE: You found a place?
MARY:　　　　　　I got a room for nothing,
　　or pretty much. The landlord, he's a good man,
　　he's mashed on me, M'Carthy –
JOE:　　　　　　　　　M'Carthy?
　　Miller's Court, you mean, in Dorset Street?

MARY: Down the road.

JOE: Lord no, we can't live there,
    Marie, it's common dwellings,
    it's doss-houses, it's slumland –

MARY: It's three shilling,
    Joe, for a whole room.

JOE: Marie, listen.
    I am a foreman, in a waged position,
    at Billingsgate fish market, in the heart
    of a great city –

MARY: Yes, so all that wage
    comes in each week, and what's the rent? Three shilling,
    haddock man, we'll have a fortune over!
    Just you and me. I took this place myself.
    I took it, Joe!

JOE: I heard you.

MARY: To be with you
    somewhere, where I have friends, you know, blonde friends,
    Joe. The Grays Inn Road,
    that's China, Joe, up there, it's not my world.

JOE: You've seen the world.

MARY: I have. Three shilling, Joe!

JOE: I hear you. Doss-it Street…

MARY: Whitechapel, the World!

Scene Seven

The Alley / Millers Court.

MARY: (*Sings.*) *If you were the only girl in the world*
                    and I was the only boy
                    nothing else would matter in the world today
                    we would go on loving in the same old way…

    Little Marie's been slaving at the Ringers.
    I had a workload, so they made me foreman,
    in a waged position.
    Tonight I thought of walking on the streets
    all night but I came home because my Joseph,
    not *his* Joseph, not even Joseph's Joseph,

lives here, so I'm here. And now I think
we'll have a song, we'll have a goodnight song.
(*She gets into the bed without undressing. He stays at the
table.*)

(*Sings.*) *Iesu tirion, gwel yn awr*
   Blentyn bach yn plygu i lawr;
   Wrth fy ngwendid trugarha,
   Paid a'm gwrthod, Iesu da.

That's my little prayer. Marie Jeanette.
Forgive me, Jesus, if my Welsh is rusty.
See I was kneeling, though.

Scene Eight

Millers Court.

(*JOE comes with a box and a newspaper. Morning light.
MARY is asleep in the bed. JOE goes into the room and places
the box on the chair by the bed.*)

JOE: Marie! Marie!
MARY: No one of that name
 here…
JOE: I got you something.
 I got you something. Nature of a surprise.
MARY: Ask me to close my eyes then.
JOE: Open your eyes.
MARY: They are, they just feel closed.
JOE: I'll place it here.
 I'll place it here to wait for you.
 I'll get the fire going.
MARY: I'm asleep, Joe,
 it's going in my dream.
JOE: You're asleep?
 Then I'm asleep, and if I am I'm dreaming,
 and I can do my worst!
 (*He tries to tickle her, she curls away. He goes to the fire.*)
 See even in my dream you're my Jeanetta.
 Ma mademoiselle de Paree. You think Paree

is ready for Joe Barnett?
I see us, you and me, dancing the waltz,
or the polonaise on the avenues!
(*MARY crawls out of bed.*)
Nothing you need to do. I'm making tea.
MARY: Make tea then, I'll make water. What's this?
JOE: Nature of a surprise!
MARY: All that for me now.
Is it all the sins of the world?
JOE: I beg your pardon?
(*She goes out.*)
Things you say... Is it all the sins of the world...
You see what's in there and your thoughts may turn
on sinful matters!
MARY: (*From off.*)   Long time since they turned
on anything much else.
JOE: And don't I know it!
Don't I indeed, Marie!
(*She comes back. She sees the newspaper on the table, and looks
at it.*)
MARY: Is that the paper?
JOE: The Times, the London Times.
MARY: The *London* Times...
Who's this lucky lady?
JOE: Not so fortunate, Lord rest her soul.
(*JOE goes outside.*)
MARY: Front page of the Times, the London Times...
Princess How-de-do, then, or it's one's
been murdered. There's two ways to get your picture
featured nowadays.
(*JOE comes back in.*)
JOE: It's not no princess.
MARY: You're having a pee and there's the princess murdered.
JOE: You going to open up your present there?
MARY: Her all alone in the great Times of London.
JOE: You might say she's at peace, though that depends
on your religious notions.
(*MARY gets back into bed.*)

MARY: Is it night yet?

JOE: One might indeed propose that that there lady
abides in a warm region.

MARY: Lucky old princess.

JOE: Open the box, Marie.

MARY: Why, will it go away? Is it a dress, Joe?

JOE: It may be, it may not be.

MARY: I knew a man who liked to buy me dresses.

JOE: Did you. That's generous of the Welsh wizard.

MARY: He came from Stepney, Joe, not so much wizard
as gasworks-man.

JOE: But blessed, having you
to buy a present for. Not so blessed now
it's me who has that honour.

MARY: No not so blessed.
(*JOE brings her tea.*)

JOE: In answer to your qu-question,
the lady's not a princess. What she's been
is *savaged*, as they say.

MARY: I'm pretty hungry.
Let's go to Ringers, Joe.

JOE: It's only morning,
it's not midday.

MARY: Tell me about the princess.
Who savaged her, the king?
(*She lies back in bed. JOE reads.*)

JOE: 'Early hours of Friday…
the woman now known as Mary Ann Nichols…'

MARY: Mary Nichols? Can't be *that* Mary Nichols.

JOE: '…was known as Polly to her friends…'

MARY: Oh my.
She's nothing like her picture.
Not so pretty, Polly. What was I doing,
early hours of Friday? Sitting there…

JOE: 'A knife – ' I'll skip that part…
'possibly left-handed…' Ah, a statement:
'The police admit their belief that the three…deaths…'
Three? Have there been three? '…may be the work

of one individual. All three women were known
"unfortunates", each so very poor,
   that robbery is thought to have formed no motive...'
'Unfortunates', you know what that's a word for,
do you not, Marie?

MARY: But they're so very poor, Joe.
   Robbery forms no motive for my friendship.

JOE: I won't read you the details of the stabwounds.

MARY: Why, are they in French? All right, it's time.
   (*MARY gets out of bed.*)
   Marie's unbirthday present.

JOE: Unbirthday?

MARY: Unbirthday present. You know, Humpty Dumpty.
   In the story. Did you *ever* have a childhood?

JOE: This box will be giant-size when it's your birthday.

MARY: Why, will there be a man in it? It's a dress, Joe.

JOE: It just most certainly is!

MARY: It's a yellow dress.

JOE: It *is* that daffodil shade, for my lady.

MARY: Or was it white till reaching Dorset Street
   it blended in?

JOE: No it's true flower yellow.

MARY: Where did you get it, Joe, did they just make you
   lord of all fish commerce?

JOE: Ways and means
   for a working man, Jeanetta, ways and means.

MARY: Thank you, Joseph, I'll be sure to wear it
   at yellow moments.

JOE: Golden moments!

MARY: Golden
   intervals. Thank you.

JOE: You'll look a picture!

MARY: Will they put me in the London Times?

JOE: They better!
   (*MARY starts trying the dress on.*)

MARY: Where'd they find the lady?

JOE: What lady?
   (*She points.*)
   Her? In, in Bucks Row.

That's by Whitechapel Station. I myself
have walked there.

MARY: That's spine-chilling.
Just think. And are there other
famous ways you've trodden?

JOE: There's a notion.
They ought to search the trains.

MARY: And all the towns
that trains can take you, then the rest of England
for a man who might be possibly left handed.
There'll be a rare parade, we can line them up
on the white cliffs and (*She blows.*)
(*MARY in the dress. She starts taking it off quickly.*)

JOE: Quite beauteous.
A golden vision!

MARY: Where'd she live, the lady?
The 'unfortunate' lady.

JOE: Right! In, in Thrawl Street...
'Nothing more was known...Thrawl Street...but that
when she presented herself for her lodging
Thursday night she was turned away because
she had not got the money...' The old story.
How fearfully 'unfortunate' for Polly!

MARY: Friend of yours, was she?

JOE: Well, no, just joking...
'She was then the worse for drink, but not drunk...'

MARY: Again? The worse for drink but not drunk?
Have I been the worse for drink and not drunk?

JOE: 'And turned away laughing, saying,
"I'll soon get my doss money; see what a jolly
bonnet I've got now!"'

MARY: The better for drink?
I've been the better for drink.

JOE: 'It was dark at the time,
though there was a street-lamp shining on Bucks Row...'

MARY: My, they have a street-lamp. Do they turn
a tap to get champagne?

JOE: That'd be something.

'Deceased was lying on her back with her dress
disarranged…'

MARY:　　　　　　Professional to the end.

JOE: 'Witness felt her arm, which did seem warm
from the joints upwards, while her eyes were wide
open. Her bonnet was off her head and was lying
by her right side…'

(*While JOE rambles on, MARY goes to the pub, drinks beer,
eats bread, chats.*)

Scene Nine

The Ringers Pub.

MARY: That's good enough to make you worse for drink.
Not drunk, mind you. You hear about the murder?
I heard it, Mr Barnett got a paper,
he tried to solve the case. My Mr Barnett,
nothing gets past him. He's a fine fine man,
he stops at every comma for a sigh.
He sniffs at the full stops. He's on the case.
Last year I met him. Met him on Good Friday,
my haddock-man, he caught me in his net.
Joseph believes I'm fortunate to have him.
Fortunate, that's me.
I think I'm worse for drink, but I'm not drunk, mind,
unfortunately, I am a golden vision…
(*She gets another glass of beer.*)
Barnett has lost his job, but he doesn't know
I know it. Joe was fired
last week for stealing fish. When he leaves for work
it's to the docks he goes where he gets nothing.
Money was all we had, Billingsgate money,
Shillingsgate, Pennygate…
He doesn't know I know. He says tomorrow –

JOE: Wear the dress, I'm bringing home a banquet!

Scene Ten

Millers Court.

(*JOE has prepared a candlelit table. Wine, orange firelight.
Newspapers on the floor. MARY sits to eat. Uneasy quiet.
They speak simultaneously.*)

MARY ⎱ How do you do it –
JOE ⎰ Fellow at work today –

MARY ⎱ You first.
JOE ⎰ You first.

MARY: It's nothing, I was wondering how the fish
    lost all his bones. When we had fish for tea
    I used to choke. When I was in silk stockings
    I learnt to choke politely. Here with you,
    I've lost my choking manners.
JOE: No bones,
    it's guaranteed, roll up, stocks while they last!
MARY: You hawker, Barnett, there's a new vocation
    if you ever needed one.
JOE: If I ever did!
    My, this is grand.
MARY: It feels like someone else's
    life just started.
JOE: Somebody born lucky!
JOE: Fellow at work, he said, 'Hey Mr Barnett,
    nicer bit of haddock
    you'll never taste, old friend.'
MARY: You'll never taste
    a decent meal again? Is he some prophet?
    He's wasted at the fishhouse.
JOE: More wine,
    ma share Maria Jeanetta?
MARY: By all means,
    fair and foul, let's send it home to France.
JOE: France, your local haunt!
MARY: My local haunt. I was only there a week.
JOE: No place for ladies.

MARY: Fish lost all his bones.

JOE: My, this is grand.

MARY: It is, Joe.

(*They eat and drink.*)

I knew Dark Annie.

JOE: Who?

MARY: That woman. Mrs Chapman. In the paper.

JOE: Chapman, yes, found slaughtered.

MARY: *Mrs* Chapman,
Joe, you got no right to cut her name up.
But I knew her as Dark Annie, and she's dead now,
she's in the news and never had a thing,
Dark Annie, just a temper.
Been in a fair old scrap, last time I saw her.
Sold flowers she used to, friend of Teddy Stanley.
Poor lad, he did like Annie.

JOE: Has Mr Stanley
been through the proper channels?

MARY: What channels?

(*JOE picks up a newspaper.*)

JOE: 'The suspect Pizer (alias Leather Apron)
and the suspect Pigott (no known aliases)…'
There's all the names they've mentioned.

MARY: Some good lads
you can't ask, 'Did you slash a woman up?'
They're not from where that's done.

JOE: Today we're all
from where that's done, it's here! It's Scotland Yard
decides who's on the level.

MARY: Scotland Yard,
is it, Joe?

JOE: It's probability
they'll bring more agents in.

MARY: Sure, very good,
more agents, Joe.

JOE: They'll need to talk to you,
if you knew *Mrs* Chapman. How'd you know her?

MARY: What, are you an agent?

JOE: I could pass as!

MARY: How did I know Dark Annie? On my bootsole.
    I looked one morning and unfortunates
    were creeping east and west.
JOE: When the Yard calls
    they may require a proper yes or no,
    and nothing but the truth.
MARY: Well, in that case,
    has Scotland Yard been asking how your day was,
    Joseph, at the dockside?
    (*JOE stands and walks around, sits down again.*)
JOE: I've been, and for no reason,
    I've been and temporary,
    let off the work a time, for quite a mix-up,
    a c-case of –
MARY: A case of wine? A c-case of haddock?
JOE: Mistook identities.
MARY: What, did the man
    who stole the fish use this hand or that hand?
    Did he steal it left to right and does he use
    a jack-knife or a dagger when he guts it?
JOE: If, as it turns, I did, to all effects,
    remove the fish unwarranted, I c-can
    at least, whole-hearted like, and bold, state here
    what's done were done for none but my Marie,
    as were the dress you wear –
MARY: The dress I wear
    you had your hands on first.
JOE: What does that mean?
MARY: Ask it yourself.
JOE: I have retained some money,
    special, and there's much work to be had,
    in the daytime situations in the region
    of Shadwell Docks –
MARY: Where thousands wait all night
    to get it while we're banqueting on what?
    (*Sound of banging from above.*)
JOE: Sally's trying to sleep upstairs.
MARY: (*To the room above.*)   Try harder.
    (*Silence.*)

JOE: As I say, I have retained some funds.

MARY: *Mae gen ti un wy, does dim gen i.*
  Don't you agree? I'm going to go to Ringers,
  become the worse for drink.

JOE: You're going nowhere!

MARY: I beg your pardon, Joe?

JOE: You can't alone,
  not with Leather Apron out there.

MARY: Who?
  I thought you said he was put away with all
  his kitchen blades.

JOE: Marie,
  please stay here, please stay.

MARY: *Torrwch y dorff I Mari.*
  I'll stay here if you'll go.
  Go to the dockside, Joe, we're in the ditch
  if you don't get called on. Go to the dockside,
  somebody has to need you.

JOE: Marie, Marie...

MARY: You have retained some funds –

JOE: Let's go together,
  away, away to K-K-K-

MARY: To County Cork?

JOE: K-K-K-

MARY: To California?

JOE: To Kent, to pick the berries, in the trees,
  for harvesting, still harvesting, they are –
  Sunny days, Marie!

MARY: In California
  there's *oranges* on trees, Joe. Let's walk it.

JOE: I mean it, my idea!

MARY: It's far away,
  we don't know people there.

JOE: We don't need people.

MARY: (*Sotto voce.*) I need some people, now I do. I need
  a spell in the gaslight.

JOE: Promise me
  you'll stay here till the morning?

MARY: Oh, I promise.

    Tell Scotland Yard I promised.

    I crossed my heart, you hoped.

JOE: If anybody comes, call up to Sally,

    ask her who it is.

MARY: What if it's you,

    shall I let you in?

JOE: You'll see me

    afternoon, tomorrow, a tired man

    with shillings in both hands. Goodnight, Marie.

MARY: Goodnight.

JOE: It's foggy out.

MARY: It's foggy in.

    (*JOE goes up the alley. MARY looks in the mirror, makes up her face.*)

    Sally, you coming down?

    (*JOE comes back – at the sound of his voice MARY hides under the bed.*)

JOE: Marie, it's me, it's Joe!

    There's been a new event, out to the east,

    another like the previous, I heard them,

    on Leman Street they ran like billy-o!

    Marie? It's Joe. Marie?

    (*He goes in.*)

    (*To the room above.*) Sally, are you there? You got my Mary?

    You see her go, you gone with her? You ladies,

    you better watch yourselves…you better watch

    my Mary, or I tell you, you'll have Joe

    to reckon with as well!

    (*JOE goes out into pitch darkness.*)

    Who's there? Is someone there?

    I live near here, now, and I know the coppers.

    PC Leach and PC Thain, I know them.

    I have a stick, you know. You keep your distance…

    (*JOE lights a match. MARY has gone out and is trying to creep past.*)

    Who's that? You came before.

    Who's there?

MARY: (*Disguising her voice.*) Is your name Davy?

JOE: Barnett. I can't see you.

MARY: That's as there's no light.

JOE: You sound like someone.

    You sound like someone.

MARY: Do I sound like Mary Ann?

JOE: Mary Ann?

MARY: Am I right for the Minories?

JOE: Where are you? Are you there?

    (*Spotlight up. No one. JOE hurries off.*)

Act Two

Scene One

Millers Court.

(Dawn. Darkness, fire gone out. The room is a mess. Someone's in the bed. JOE comes to the alley, goes up to the door, knocks. He tries the door and it opens. He goes in, assumes it's Mary in the bed, then squats down by the grate to make a fire.)

JOE: You'll perish from the cold if you don't perish
    from want of care, Marie.
    This place stinks like the Ringers.
    There's only been two more. Round Mitre Square
    there's knocking on a riot. Someone's only
    torn to bits, I'm saying it straight out,
    but scarce believing it. I couldn't sleep,
    I couldn't face the docks, I don't know now
    what I can do, I wandered up and down,
    saw people running here and back and forth.
    Agent Towler, he's been drafted in,
    like, special, and he tells me,
    confidential style mind,
    knowing me for an upright class of fellow,
    'Barnett, be discreet,' but what he's saying is,
    this monster did two females in an hour.
    He savaged 'em. One hour.
    Berner Street, by some Jews' secret club.
    There's rumours flying. Someone said there's writing
    in Jewish on a wall, I think in blood, though,
    points at who it is, not pulling punches,
    but writing plain as day.
    And then there's Mitre Square, they said is cursed.
    Another whore. I call it as it is.
    Ain't seen the papers yet, but I can tell you,
    it's animal, it is, they're saying fiendish.
    There's parts of her, whole parts…

Thing is, he also tells me,
confidential style mind,
she never gave her name as what it is –
Kate something – what she gave were what he calls
a pseudo-name. The name was Mary Kelly.
He says I ought to know this, as my missus,
his words, goes sometimes by the very name
of Mary Kelly –
(*The door opens and it's MARY, exhausted, the worse for wear.
It's someone else in the bed. JOE goes to see who, but MARY
gets there first.*)

MARY: Don't wake her, will you, sweetheart?

JOE: Don't wake her, don't wake who?

MARY: Mrs Van Turney,
she's quite done in, poor lamb.

JOE: But I don't know her.

MARY: She'd do the same for you, and you look weary.
(*MARY covers the 'sleeper' and sits on the edge of the bed.*)

JOE: You mean from number eight?

MARY: Not any more,
she's not, she's from no number, her address
is nil, it's nought, it's open to the skies.

JOE: Let her go home to them then.

MARY: Hush, my dear.

JOE: Your dear, your dear, your sweetheart.

MARY: All those things. You know there's been a killing?

JOE: Wrong, that's quite fallacious.

MARY: Is it really,
well, that's news to everyone, there hasn't.
That's good news for the victim,
her kipping in the mortuary, I'm pleased
she's made a quick recovery.

JOE: Not one,
but two. Both in an hour.
Two female persons slaughtered last night, sweetheart.

MARY: There's been two killed?

JOE: No. Killed there's been now five,
all told, but two last night. Unfortunates.

MARY: You think so, Joe?

JOE: I know so.

MARY: My dress,
    it's got itself dismantled. It's beyond
    repair, even for Julie.

JOE: And who's Julie?

MARY: This is Julie.

JOE: Shall we rouse this Julie?

MARY: No, she's too fallacious, and why trouble,
    this dress is beyond her help.

JOE: Oh, she's a seamstress,
    is she, that her profession?

MARY: You never know what's going to need a thread,
    my dearest, not these days.

JOE: Your friends are whores.
    Mrs Albrook, Mrs Harvey, this one –

MARY: What happened to their first names, were they found
    with all their insides out? Now you must call me
    Mrs Kelly. Sorry, slipped my mind,
    my maiden name's not one your tongue can manage.
    What can it manage? Talking it can manage.
    Or am I being fallacious?

JOE: As for that,
    your name, your maiden name, your name's been used
    in an intriguing fashion just last night,
    I have it on authority from one
    deep down involved –

MARY: You see you missed your time
    to deep down be involved, you missed the boat
    with me on board –

JOE: I missed it? I miss nothing,
    Mary Jane –

MARY: Can you help me?
    Can you get me out of here?
    You got a fish for me that I can swim with?
    Got me a florin, Barnett?
    Got me a gilded carriage to the fruit fields?

JOE: I have retained some funds, but now it's scarce
    enough –

MARY: We're thirty shillings
down on rent. Last night I saw M'Carthy,
he said we had a week. I talked him back
and now we've till November.

JOE: November…

MARY: Good time to hit the old Kent Road, eh Joseph,
now all our clothes are curtains in the pawnshop?

JOE: Thirty? Thirty shillings?

MARY: I'm so tired.
She's going to help us out.

JOE: Who is, that woman there? We don't have need
of anything she's got.

MARY: She's got five shillings,
shh, so yes we might do.

JOE: I'll get money.
I'll settle with M'Carthy.

MARY: Think he'd sooner
bargain with my species.

JOE: Promise me
you don't do what these women do.

MARY: I promise
I don't do what these women do. (*Sotto voce.*) I *can't*
do half of it, I swear.

JOE: Now, wake her up,
and gentle is in order, let this lady
know she is not welcome –

MARY: She is welcome.

JOE: You mean until she wakes.

MARY: I mean until I don't mean.

JOE: In our place.

MARY: In my place. It's in my name,
remember.

JOE: Marie, Marie…

MARY: You know that much.

JOE: How can we hold together with this woman
lying there?

MARY: How can we eat without
you earning?

JOE: You could pawn your dresses…
MARY: Right.
    I could go naked, but my selfishness
    won't let me, Joe, and pride, my shocking pride.
    I pride myself, it's all I do all day.
JOE: I can't get taken on, down by the docks,
    and when I reach the gate I'm fit to faint
    with hanging round. I say I were a foreman
    at Billingsgate, I say so, and their eyes
    look through me like I'm nothing.
MARY: Go naked,
    they'll notice you, let's both do…
    I'm tired as he must be, the killing fellow.
    Quite a night's work. I mean, compared to yours.
    They pay him by the pint, you reckon? Funny,
    to think, he must be sleepy.
JOE: I won't stay
    if she won't go.
MARY: All right, but if your seams
    fall apart, my dear, you come to us,
    we're legends with the needle.
JOE: You mean that?
    You mean that?
MARY: Trousers, jackets…
JOE: You mean about me going, Mary Jane?
MARY: *Mary Jane?* Gone English on me, have you?
    Mary Jane. Is that another pet-name?
    A sign of love, that is. I knew a man
    who used to –
JOE: Spare me tales of the old country.
MARY: Morganstone, he used to. Mind you,
    it helped he could pronounce it,
    get his tongue around it.
JOE: I'm leaving now. And not as I'm accustomed,
    with coming back and all, and saying sorry,
    I'm leaving for the Grays Inn Road, that's right,
    in case you haven't understood, I'm leaving.
MARY: That's three times, Joe, say it another forty
    I'll take a lively interest.

JOE: I'm leaving,
   and that's the final saying, no returns.
   And these are times with someone on the loose
   who's animal, a species of his kind!
   I ought to stay but look at me, bag's packed
   and shipshape. You ought to go where I go.
MARY: Will *you* be there, where you go?
JOE: Will I – always!
MARY: Then I'll stay here where I am.
JOE: Right. You do that.
   I'm stretching out my hand but you won't take it.
   So I'll take my leave!
MARY: Don't wake Mrs Van Turney.
   She needs her seven hours.
JOE: I'm out the door.
   I'm walking down the street!
   (*JOE goes.*)
MARY: That's not a job they pay you for.
JOE: (*From off.*)   I know.
   At least I'm going somewhere.
MARY: Go to hell then.
JOE: (*From off.*) After you, I insist!
   (*JOE breaks a window.*)
   That ought to wake the lady!

Scene Two

The Alley.

(*MARY drunk.*)

MARY: (*Sings.*) *...So while life does remain*
                 In memoriam I'll retain
                 This small violet I picked from mother's grave...

   Why'd you pick it, Mary, leave it be,
   you stupid child! I'm sorry, mam, it's only
   a violet I plucked when but a boy.
   You're a girl, you stupid child. And you're dead, mam,
   that's both of us been cleared by Scotland Yard.

You left-boned or right-boned? Ah, then suspicion
lights upon you, mam. You're a fool girl.
I sound the worse for drink, but I'm not drunk.
I won't die here, for sure, I'll crawl the miles
home if I feel edgy,
we'll ride the train together. – Me and Barnett?
Is that your act, some comedy? I'll book you,
right? in the penny gaffs. You'll have 'em screaming.
Tell the one about the B-B-Barnetts!
No, no. No, Morganstone,
Morganstone. He knows me,
Morganstone. We'll be the talk of Stepney,
us women of Whitechapel. They'll be coming
sooner than you know,
in hundreds from the gasworks
and lead us from this place. Poor Joe was at it,
let's walk to Kent, let's pick whatever berries
grow where there's no people. I myself
am leaving, you're all coppers…

Act Three

Scene One

Millers Court.

(*JOE returns in a new suit.*)

JOE: Like old times, Marie. Just passing through.
    Looked in at the Ringers, my.
    Quiet as the proverbial... The lads
    all blaming Jack for business. Jack's the name
    been settled on. Those letters, now there's hundreds.
    's in case you want...some pictures...   (*The newspaper.*)
    Street's so quiet too. It's like he's made
    a Sunday of the whole wide world, has Jack.
MARY: Welcome to the beer-shop.
JOE: How's that, love?
MARY: Mary's Beer-shop, Mary's Arms, we call it,
    or Sally's Arms, or Julie's Head. We three
    we work an honest day.
JOE: You do your – threading works.
MARY: We do our works.
    We're legends of the needle.
JOE: So I hear,
    you and your seamstresses.
    Marie, I were passing through. I wish I had
    a shilling for you, but it's not been good.
    Bought on tick,
    this whole new rig of mine, would you believe?
    Pay it back next spring. I got some pennies,
    rental funds. So I'm sorry,
    this call is well, it's social. Marie Jeanette...
    The lads at Ringers say the local girls,
    gone to the workhouse sharpish. Rather that
    than hang about for Jack.

MARY: That's as they can't
   do stitches. How would a gentleman survive
   without a girl attending to his stitches…

JOE: I'm only saying.

MARY: What though.
   'Get to the workhouse, darling.'

JOE: Not in your case.
   In your case there's a place.

MARY: Not here there's not.
   I'm here. I can be found here. People know
   how to find me.

JOE: Who knows how to find you?
   Who knows how to find you?
   Morganstone? My my.
   You think he'll come and find you, come and fetch you
   out of here?

MARY: 'Get to the workhouse, sweetheart.'

JOE: You're drunk again.

MARY: I am the worse for drink,
   those things are very different.

   (*JOE sees something outside and goes to the window.*)

JOE: Someone's out there.
   Stay there.

MARY: Because there's someone?
   It's London. I'll remain here till all London
   floats by, shall I?

JOE: What's your business, friend?
   He's moving off. He's seen I have a purpose.

MARY: Sharper eyes than me.

JOE: You know that fellow?

MARY: Oh, that's Tom.

JOE: Who's Tom?

MARY: He's thick with Dick and Harry,
   you know, they'll be along soon.

JOE: Thomas what?
   I ought to report his movements.

MARY: God help us,
   he's here for Julia, what are you thinking?
   He needs his collars loosened.

JOE: Well indeed.
    This is, then, under law,
    the house in which we lived, and loved –
MARY: Sweet Jesus.
JOE: A house of prostitution.
MARY: It's a house
    that has a roof and walls but we three witches
    sleep in our own cauldron.
JOE: This is my offer,
    made to you. You put these – ladies – out,
    and I return.
MARY: You mean, come down from heaven?
    Give up the Grays Inn Road?
JOE: This work – this life
    is dragging you to hell.
MARY: Oh there's a hell?
    What's this then, Mr fish man?
JOE: What you don't realise is that there's nothing,
    Marie Jeanette, not anything I won't
    forgive in you, not one thing I can't say
    you do that but I – I reiterate,
    love you – and may well furthermore forgive.
    What others may term *sins* –
MARY: Oh, keep watch, you might burn,
    a light's gone on above your head. Caught you!
    I thought it was new street lights. Thought you'd found
    a job worth doing.
JOE: Here's another one.
MARY: Where?
JOE: Across the court. (*To the man.*) For Mrs Harvey,
    No? Mrs Van Turney?
MARY: Don't know that one.
JOE: Sorry! The whores are gone! Marie, you tell him.
    Come on, come to the window.
MARY: No I won't.
JOE: There's just Miss Kelly here. Come to the window.
MARY: (*To JOE.*) Oh, damn you, go away.
JOE: (*Thinks it's to the man.*) You hear that loud and clear?
    I think he's got the picture.

MARY: Oh I'm hungry.

JOE: I know. I'm hungry too.

MARY: (*Sotto voce.*)   But I don't chuck
    your dinner in the Thames.

JOE: These are dark times.

MARY: *Paid a'm gwrthod, Iesu da.*

JOE: Indeed, indeed.

MARY: I'll go, but when I go
    it's far away I'm going.

JOE: I can take you.
    There's nothing I won't do. I think I've shown that
    by coming back to help a friend in need.

MARY: Who? Me? You can't go where I'm going.
    You don't know where it is.

JOE: Marie, they say the night the two were done,
    Eddowes, the second one, gave out her name
    was Mary Kelly, and the inquest stated
    she often went as Kelly, as her boyfriend
    shared that name. My contact, Agent Towler,
    he seemed to think that any Mary Kelly
    hereabouts –

MARY: Oh he's killing for the name,
    is he? that's smart. I'm changing mine to Barnett.

JOE: You ought to be more watchful.

MARY: Oh I'm watchful,
    love, I'm full of watching.

JOE: Someone else.

MARY: The candlestick-maker, no?

JOE: Don't think so. He looks well-to-do. Stay back.
    (*MARY goes to see.*)
    One of them West End slummers.
    What are you nodding for? He's nodding too.
    You know that man.

MARY: Sweet Jesus.

JOE: You want me to run him off?
    He's…he's here for you then, is he?
    He's your – he's your – your gent.
    A better, rather a better –

class of type, I wager…well, it's done,
the truth is out, the core of it, the heart
I must endure and shall, indeed, endure,
is in the open. Where are the other women?
I shan't leave you alone. I remain Christian.
I shan't –

MARY: You have to, Barnett.
It's how it works.

JOE: That's it, then.
Well I'll take a look at him, I will. I'll wait
same spot where he were waiting, till the deeds
are, as it were…

MARY: No don't.
Go far away, there's nobody to wait for.

JOE: Transactions will take place, and I shall then
return.

MARY: Don't do that either.
Transactions never end.

JOE: Well. That's as may be.
I shall, indeed, move on. I am most glad
to see you, Miss K-Kelly. Well. Good evening.

Scene Two

The Alley.

(JOE is outside the room, rehearsing what he wants to say.)

JOE: Stop there, my name's Joe Barnett,
I am this lady's friend, and I insist –
I demand that at this moment…
All right, that's it, you dirtbag!
You are a wretched savage. Wretched dirtbag!
This woman is…my own. I won't stand by
and let the likes of you,
come in here, besmirching – here besmirching
a beautiful young rose…
Marie, leave it to Joe. You stand aside.
(JOE prepares to enter. The clock is striking ten.)

Marie? It's me, it's Joe.
(*MARY can be heard laughing inside.*)
What are you laughing at? Can you hear me?
Marie? It's me, it's Joe.
Marie? Marie Jeanette?
(*MARY stops laughing. The light goes out in the room.*)
Marie, who's that still there?
I know I can be heard.
I know you can both hear me.
(*MARY and a man's voice, both laughing, then hushing. JOE turns away.*)

Scene Three

Millers Court / The Ringers Pub.

(*Pitch darkness. MARY screams. Breathing sound. JOE comes back, in spotlight.*)

JOE: Young copper, quite excitable, don't think
    he knew whom he were talking to. He said
    a telegram's went round to every station.
    Quote: 'The woman is simply cut to pieces.'
    I asked him who the victim was, I always
    took a lively interest. And the copper
    told me Millers Court and I said the number
    and he said the number with me. I was –
    required to view this – Quote: 'I have seen the body
    and identify it by the ear and eyes,
    which are the only parts I…' Unquote.
    It was…the middle of the afternoon.
    Remember thinking what would she be up to?
    Thinking – this day on I'll never let her
    wander off, I'd all her every moments
    be beside her –
    (*MARY suddenly gets out of bed.*)

MARY: Could you hang these up,
    they crease.

JOE: Like I was there when she was waking,
    Like I was who she woke with.

MARY: Mustn't let me.
   Mustn't let me drink again. I blame you
   for how I feel.
JOE: You can, you can blame me,
   I should have stopped you, shouldn't I?
MARY: Should you?
   Who are you?
JOE: Well, I'm him you slept besides
   one morning.
MARY: You're a blur. I've seen you somewhere.
JOE: Somewhere's where I went.
MARY: I'm going somewhere.
   It'll have to be the Ringers, or Lord knows
   how long I'll hold together. You coming?
JOE: Nowhere I'd rather be.
MARY: Nowhere's exactly
   where I'd rather be.
JOE: With me?
MARY: With you?
   Who are you, the Sandman? You wait here.
   I'll fetch some milk and make us tea, I'll be
   the woman you all want. My but it's bright now.
   I haven't eyes for this.
JOE: She goes again,
   but I won't let her out of sight. This time
   I go there too, I wait / for her –
MARY: / Will you pipe down?
   I'm on my way to work, you know.
JOE: I saw him,
   in the firelight, for a second, and I hoped –
   seeing him with you, I hoped he *was* him,
   Jack, in there, because my poor man's heart
   said Joe's who loves you, see?
MARY: Is there any hope
   of being served in here, or have I vanished
   and no one's saying?
JOE: No, no worries, Ginger.
MARY: A half a glass

I think is all I'm up for, love. I've been
drinking so much lately.

JOE: Half a glass
for Ginger.

MARY: Here it comes across the fields.
Into my arms. I've company, you know.

JOE: You do? That Mr Barnett? He seemed nice.

MARY: Did he? No, not him. Somebody new.

JOE: Share it with me, Ginger?

MARY: Have to drink this,
then I'm so well it's frightening, one sip,
I'm royal material.

JOE: That Morganstone
you always talked about?

MARY: I don't remember.
Somebody new. Somebody going to help me.
I've been considering a move from here.

JOE: We're all considering that one, love.

MARY: Here goes…
My arm won't lift it, man. My head is saying:
'Down it, you'll be fine…'
My arm is saying: 'Enough!'

JOE: Where would you go to?
Home to Wales?

MARY: Home across the water.
In a boat at dawn we leave, my dad and me.
He's pointing out the points of land, the clifftops,
they're disappearing, and I see small people
waving from them, waiting for the boat
all morning just to wave. I can't drink this.
Maybe a sip. There's nobody who knows me
waiting back there. Then again, I leave
London, who'll be waving?

JOE: I'll be waving,
Ginger, you're an excellent customer!

MARY: Now there's a thing to be. There's a profession.

JOE: Down the hatch.

MARY: Oh Christ.

JOE: Is there any message?

MARY: Message?

JOE: For any fellow?

MARY: I'm in a boat, with dad. I dwell abroad.

JOE: I'll think of you there, Ginger. I at least
    will be one waving from the cliffs of London!
    (*MARY goes out unsteadily to the street.*)

MARY: (*Sings.*) *She was a sweet little dicky-bird...*
    (*MARY crouches and is sick. JOE makes his way to the bed to*
    wait for her.)

JOE: Nothing in her life
    so bad as what I did, to see her there,
    with him, and walk away. Now I'm always walking.
    I walked away from, well, from what the coppers
    showed me, that's their job. Remember saying
    look what a mess been made... But she needed that,
    that – stuff God made of her, did he not know
    she needed it? It was like – a breed of dog,
    that never once been cared for,
    were staring at me and no act of ours
    is sheltered from its eyes...
    (*MARY goes back to the room.*)

MARY: Sweetheart. Can't imagine what I went for.

JOE: Milk, but I don't mind. I'll have my tea
    black in a while, not now.

MARY: I think I need
    to sleep it off and all the Lord Mayor's horses
    will have to do without me. Can you stay?

JOE: Of course I will. I made the fire nice like.

MARY: My head's all spinning round. I'm trying to think
    how ever on earth I came here. I have nothing,
    sweetheart, I have you, but I don't know you.
    You could be the first man, or the last man.
    Thinking of you just makes the world go faster.
    I'm trying to find what slows it down. A song
    might slow it down but I don't have the breath to.
    (*He tucks her up, and puts a sheet over her face.*)

JOE: Feel that, it's cool, now you can think yourself
    most anywhere you like. You're happy there,

you're in full cry. Don't have a mind with room
for what was done to you. No one should have.
At least if I'd been him who did that deed
I'd know the earth held nothing that was worse,
then I could close my eyes and all be darkness,
and not these twisting shapes I tend to see.
These images I made are my day's work,
each morning till the time
I hear Death knock. Mind I don't break his ribs
with hugging him that day!